Celtic MYTHOLOGY

*The Nature and Influence of Celtic Myth – from
Druidism to Arthurian Legend*

Ward Rutherford

CORONET

This edition published in Great Britain in 2015 by Coronet
An imprint of Hodder & Stoughton
An Hachette UK company

1

Copyright © Ward Rutherford 1987

A CIP catalogue record for this title is available from the British Library

ISBN 978 1 473 60628 9
Ebook ISBN 978 1 473 60627 2

Printed and bound by CPI Group (UK) Ltd, Croydon, CR0 4YY

Hodder & Stoughton policy is to use papers that are natural, renewable and
recyclable products and made from wood grown in sustainable forests. The
logging and manufacturing processes are expected to conform to the
environmental regulations of the country of origin.

Hodder & Stoughton Ltd
Carmelite House
50 Victoria Embankment
London EC4Y 0DZ
www.hodder.co.uk

Contents

LIST OF ILLUSTRATIONS

(Between pages 75 and 82)

The Gundestrup Cauldron.

The horned god Cernunnos.

Frieze of warriors from the Gundestrup Cauldron.

The Aylesford Bucket.

A typical Celtic torc.

Iron-age hill-fort.

A stone head from Gloucester.

Annual well dressing ceremony in Derbyshire.

The Abbots Bromley 'stag men.'

'Gorsedd of the Bards of Kernow.'

The crowning of the 'Archdruid' at the Welsh Eisteddfod.

PRONOUNCING GLOSSARY
OF CELTIC NAMES

It is, of course, possible to render Celtic place and personal names phonetically, but the difference between these and the spellings likely to be encountered in other versions is so great that one may not be recognizable as the other. For example, it would need some ingenuity to realise that a name written as 'Dalna' in its phonetic form was that written 'Dealgnaid' in sources which chose to remain closer to the original. For this reason I have tried to stick to the Celtic versions. At the same time, it must be understood (1) that the phonetic forms offered here are no more than a broad guide to pronunciation, and (2) that there are no consistent rules for, particularly, Gaelic spellings. The name which I have rendered as 'Cu Chulainn' can with equal correctness be spelt 'Cuchulainn', 'Cu Chulaind', 'Cuchullin' and in several other ways. Nor do I claim that the following list is exhaustive. Only those names which occur most frequently have been included.

Note: italicised syllables are stressed

Aoife: *Eef*-ay
Ailill: *Al*-ill
Amergin: Am-*org*-in
Aneirin: An-*oi*-rin
Annwn: *An*-noon
Annwvyn: An-*oov*-an
Arawn: A-*rown*
Arianrhod: Aree-*an*-rod
Badb: Baav
Balor: *Bah*-lorr
Beltaine: *Bail*-tin
Bile: *Bee*-leh
Blodeuwedd: Blod-*ai*-weth
Bodb: Bov
Cathbhad: *Cath*-va
Cernunnos: *Ker*-noon-os
Cerridwen: Ker-*id*-wen
Cian: *Kee*-an
Conare: Kon-ar-*ee*
Conchobhar: *Con*-ah-khar
Cuailnge: Cooley

Cu Chulainn: *Coo Hool*-in
Curoi: Cur-*ree*
Dealgnaid: *Dal*-na
Dechtine: *Det*-een-eh
Derdriu: *Deer*-dree
Diancecht: *Jan*-kett
Diarmait: *Der*-mot
Diwrnach: *Dur*-nakh
Dyfed: Duv-*it*
Emer: Ev-*air*
Eochaid: *Yo*-hee
Etain: *Ett*-an
Evrawg: Eff-*rowg*
Ferdia: Fer-*dee*-ah
Fianchuive: Fee-an-*kheev*-eh
Finn mac Cumhail: Finmac
    Cumm-al
Finnabair: Finn-*av*-eer
Fuamnach: *Foo*-na
Gabra: *Gow*-ra
Gilvaethy: Ghil-*vath*-ee

Goronwy: Gor-*on*-wee
Gwalchmei: Goo-*alkh*-meh
Gwawl: *Goo*-owl
Gwent Ys Coed: Gwent uss Coit
Gwrhyr: *Gur*-heer
Gwydion: Gwud-*yon*
Gwynedd: Gwin-*eth*
Gwynhwyvar: *Gwin*-hwee-var
Iolo Morganwg: Ee-*oll*-o Mor-*gahn*-ook
Kulhwch: *Kil*-hookh
Law Gyffes: Low Guff-*ez*
Llasar Laes Gyngwyd: *Hlass*-ar Lyze *Gung*-wud
Lleu: Hlye
Llevelys: Hlev-*ell*-iss
Lludd: Hlooth
Llyr: Hleer
Loeg: Leekh
Lugh: Lookh
Mabinogion: Ma-bin-*og*-ion
Macha: Mah-kha
Mag Tuan: Moy *Too*-ra
Mallolwch: Ma-*hlol*-lukh
Manawyddan: Man-*ow*-eeth-an
March: Markh
Mathonwy: Math-*on*-wee
Mebd: Maev
Menw ap Teirnaedd: Menoo ap Tair-noo-*ayth*
Mider: *Meeth*-er
Mile: Mee-leh
Miodhchaoin: *Mee*-than
Morrigan: *Mor*-rig-ahn
Myrddin: *Mer*-thin
Niamh: *Nee*-av
Nuada: *Noo*-da
Oengus: Engus
Oisin: Ush-een
Pryderi: Prid-*er*-ree
Pwyll: Pwill
Rhiannon: Hree-*ah*-non
Rhonabwy: *Hron*-ahv-wy
Sadb: Shahv
Samain: *Shah*-vin
Scathach: *Skah*-thakh
Sidh: Shoe
Sualdam: *Sool*-dam
Tain Bo Cuailnge: Tahn Bo Cooley
Taliessin: Tal-*yess*-in
Tarbfeis: *Tar*-vaysh
Teirnon Twyrvliant: Tair-*non* Turv-*lee*-ant
Tir na n'Og: Teer nahn Ock
Tuan mac Cahill: Toon mac *Car*-il
Tuatha De Danann: Tootha Day *Dah*-nan
Tuirenn: *Teer*-enn
Twrc Trwyth: Turkh *Troo*-ith
Uath mac Imoman: Ooth mac Immoman
Ysbaddaden: Liss-path-*ad*-an

FOREWORD TO CELTIC MYTHOLOGY

Ward Rutherford's *Celtic Mythology* is a classic and justly so. The sub-title is a key to the way the book works: 'The Nature and Influence of Celtic Myth, from Druidism to Arthurian Legend.' Despite it's comparatively short extent it packs an impressive amount of material into its 176 pages, discussing Druids, the structure of Celtic myth and legend as it appears in the mythological writings of the Irish and Welsh, and the first stirrings of what would become the Matter of Britain – the Arthurian Legends. This makes the book particularly valuable, as there are still few that approach this complex subject.

Despite the advances in our knowledge of the subject made in the years since Rutherford's book first appeared, there is much here that stands up well in the face of these recent discoveries. It paints a brilliant portrait of the Celtic world and the way the people of those distant times interpreted the world around them though the creation of myths and legends. Above all Rutherford avoids the tricky matter of interpretation, which makes his book all the more useful, leaving those who read it today free to draw their own conclusions.

Here you will find what little information is available on the Druids, and details of the huge literature, dating from the 17th century, in which these few scattered remarks are used as the basis of a reconstructed belief system that holds good to the present.

Another important aspect is the spiritual background to the myths. This explores the nature and qualities of the Celtic pantheon, which in many ways parallels that of the Classical world, but with its own unique and distinctive twist.

Rutherford also deals with the other important strand of Celtic myth - the Otherworld. So much material has survived about this from Native British and Irish sources that we can see at once how important it was to the people we have come to know as the Celts. It offers a key to understanding their beliefs and traditions, which though they may seem far away from us now, nonetheless have much to tell us.

This aspect – how so many people have found meanings in these intricate stories and mythic doorways, is dealt with towards the end of the book in a most insightful way, and Rutherford touches also upon the rich heritage of materials as they have reappeared and influenced contemporary writers such as Dylan Thomas and J. R. R. Tolkien.

If you are looking for a good basic book on Celtic Mythology, unvarnished and accurate, you need look no further. Rutherford's books, which include works on Shamanism, Druidry, and the teachings of Pythagoras, are well written, honest and unfussy. He wears his extensive knowledge lightly and writes clearly and directly. It's very good to see this book back in print.

John Matthews

— PART I —

THE
WORLD
OF THE
CELTS

Chapter 1

THE INFLUENCE OF CELTIC MYTH

The mythology of the Celts can justly be claimed as one of the jewels of the European cultural heritage.

It is, to begin with, a supreme literary achievement. Particularly in the Irish stories, abundance of incident and liveliness of characterisation shine through even the late, decayed, and often bowdlerised versions that have come down to us.

They show, too, a wide range of mood. There is comedy, as for instance when King Ailill, discovering his queen extending what the Celts euphemistically called 'the friendship of the thighs' to her champion Fergus, symbolically exchanges his steel sword for one of wood. In the Irish *Bricriu's Feast*, the character of the title, as notorious a joker and mischief-maker as the Norse Loki, separately tells each of the three greatest beauties of Ulster that if she comes first to his feast, she will be queen of the province thereafter. He has so arranged matters that all arrive at precisely the same moment. As they enter the first forecourt of his palace they are models of ladylike decorum, lifting dainty feet in measured tread. At the next their gait becomes quicker. By the third it is a stride, then a run. By the time they reach his door their skirts are hitched up over their hips.

There are moments of supreme psychological insight. When Cu Chulainn becomes besotted with the sidh-woman Fand, his wife Emer, discovering it, pleads that 'What's new is bright; what's familiar is dull' and reminds him of their happy past lives together. Her plea moves Fand herself to abandon her lover, though she knows she will mourn his loss forever.

Some love scenes are more explicit, for, as the French Celticist Jean Markale says, the Celtic poet uses his characters as the means of expressing the erotic without prudery or inhibition. When Cu Chulainn catches a glimpse of Emer's breasts over her dress the first time they meet, he is impelled to comment: 'I see a sweet country there – a place I could rest my weapon.' In *Bricriu's Feast* the poet urges that 'lively naked women with fine, white, pointed breasts' should welcome the warriors home from the fray, that there should be not only fresh water for them to bathe in and good ale for them to drink, but that beds should be made ready, too.

Nor is it one sided. More than in any other literature, women, too, were recognised as having sexual desire. The breathtakingly lovely Derdriu –

she of the Sorrows – can curse, writhe, and roll on the ground in amorous madness when deprived of her lover.

Derdriu is the exemplar of another theme: the peril of beauty. Such is hers that the Druid Cathbad warns her at birth that it would bring sorrow and the death of heroes. So it proved, though her ageing husband, King Conchobhar, has her sequestered from the world in a remote peasant's hut.

There is, besides, pathetic irony, as when Cu chulainn kills his only son by Aife, daughter of the Amazon Scathach, or when he finds himself pitted in single combat with Ferdia, his fellow-student in the martial arts. Forced to kill his old friend, he carries his corpse to the burial place there to lament over him:

All play, all sport,
until Ferdia came to the ford.
I thought beloved Ferdia
would live forever after me
– yesterday, a mountain-side;
today, nothing but a shade . . .

Of course, one can always speak of great literature as 'living,' but there is a special way in which Celtic myth has remained alive.

In the 1870s Sir John Rhys began collecting Welsh and Manx folklore. He was neither the first nor the last to do so. The Revd Martin Martin did the same in the Western Isles of Scotland in the early eighteenth century. What distinguished Rhys was both his academic credentials – he was professor of Celtic at Oxford and later principal of Jesus College – and his thoroughness. He came across dozens of folk-stories of Other World hunts, magic islands, underwater cities, abductions by Other World beings, and similar prodigies all of which are to be found in the mythology, but which, for his informants, were intimately and vividly linked with the places in which they lived. Many claimed to have had personal experience of such things, or to know those who had.

Often, during Rhys's researches, a mythical character would turn up as a kind of next door neighbour. He was told by an elderly blacksmith how an old house called Castellmarch in Cardigan Bay had at one time been the home of a man so intemperate that a disgruntled servant had run away to join a man-of-war. The man succeeded in persuading its captain to anchor in the roadsteads of the bay and turn his ship's guns on the house, as proof of which the locals would show visitors what purported to be bullets.

Pressed by Rhys, the old man reluctantly admitted to an aspect of the story to which he himself gave no credence: it was said that the evil owner of Castellmarch had ass's ears. There are, in fact, two mythological equine-eared characters, one of whom is the cuckolded king in the story of Tristan and Isolt, whose name is given by the medieval storytellers as 'Mark.' This is plainly a misreading of the Welsh 'March,' which means 'a steed' and which is present as a suffix in the name 'Castellmarch.' It was explained to Rhys as being due to the fact horses had once been stabled on the estate. The old blacksmith probably knew nothing of Tristan, Isolt, or King 'Mark,' but wooden-built men-of-war were still being used by the Royal Navy in his lifetime, so he was telling, as if the horse-eared property-owner had been a recent neighbour, a story whose true antecedents go far back into Celtic paganism.

In any case, as the location of the Tristan story is usually taken to be Cornwall rather than Wales, the displacement is occurring not only in time but also in space This, too, is far from unusual and is further evidence of how far the mythology was regarded as a common Celtic heritage. One finds the same thing with other stories in the Arthurian cycle. Not only are they known and told across the entire European continent and even on the far shores of the Mediterranean and Aegean, but they have been 'adopted' by the inhabitants of widely separated areas, who solemnly claim theirs as the site of this or that incident. In the Middle Ages, Cornish and Breton monks would come to blows over just such issues. Even modern Bretons will assure you that the Forest of Broceliande and the Valley of No Return lie within the purlieus of their province, and they are even shown on some maps.

In Savoy and round Lake Geneva is an area where Arthurian place-names abound. There is a story of a woodcutter who encountered a hunting-party at a spot called Mont du Chat. They identified themselves as members of Arthur's court and invited him back to their palace, where he was regally fed, entertained, and offered hospitality which included the favours of a beautiful woman. He awoke to find himself lying uncomfortably on a pile of firewood. The vanishing castle occurs in the Irish story of 'The Birth of Cu Chulainn.'

And as to the king's tomb, it has been sited in places as far apart as Edinburgh and Mount Etna. Nor is this the sole Sicilian connection. A species of phantom island sometimes seen off its coast is described as 'Morgan le Fay's' island.

The original transmitters of this material on the continent were those British nobles and their households who, in the fifth century, began settling in what was then Neustria and later was to become known as Brittany or Petit Bretagne, to distinguish it from the main island, or Grand Bretagne. None of their original material has survived, but there are allusions in the work of medieval European writers which hint at material lost in the British versions.

By the eleventh century Arthurian incidents were even being incorporated into church architecture as far south as Italy. A sculpture on an archivolt over the north doorway of Modena Cathedral, north-west of Bologna, shows the deliverance of a woman named Winlogee from her fortress-prison. Her rescuers are four knights identified as Artus, Isdernus, Galvaginus, and Che. It is plain who is intended. 'Artus' can only be Arthur; 'Galvaginus,' Gawain, while 'Che' would be a logical Italian transliteration of Kai, Arthur's seneschal, and, as R. S. Loomis points out, 'Winlogee' is Guinevere, the form being a compromise between the Breton 'Winlowen' and the French 'Guinloie.' With slight differences the incident portrayed occurs in two early versions of the legends, Durmart le Gallois and the Vulgate Lancelot.

Among those who made enthusiastic use of the legends were the twelfth-century troubadours of southern France whose chansons were soon to contain more material drawn from the Arthurian legend than from any other single source. By the twelfth century they had carried it into the Po valley, once itself a Celtic region. Here they established such a vogue that, as several charters of the times show, 'Arthur' and 'Gawain' became popular as boys' names.

In the thirteenth and fourteenth centuries jousts and feastings, believed by their participants to be a continuation of Arthurian custom, were held annually at locations as far apart as Acre in Palestine, Prague in Bohemia, Saragossa in Spain, Falkirk in Scotland, Magdeburg in Germany, and Tournai in France.

It is its wide distribution that sets Celtic mythology apart from any other. That of the Greeks, splendid as it is, belongs indisputably to its Aegean homeland and, insofar as there is rivalry for the venues of this or that event, it is within the purlieus of the Hellenic world. The abduction of Persephone by Hades may have occurred at Eleusis in Attica or at Hermionis in the Peloponnese, as the inhabitants of each claim; no one suggests it took place beyond these confines.

Much of Celtic myth as we have it was intended to be sung, or at any rate chanted, to the strains of the harp. It was, in other words, epic poetry. Accustomed to reading them either in their prose retellings or in the metrical versions of Macpherson's spurious Ossianic poems or Tennyson in his Idylls of the King, admirable in itself, we can lose sight of the starker lines of the originals, whose austerity makes their metaphor all the more telling.

> Cold, cold,
> how cold is Lugh's great plain this night,
> the snow is higher than the hills,
> the buck finds no more food . . .
> or
> The treasure of her teeth
> is winter snow . . .

One is reminded of Old English poetry as for instance in:

> Cuckoo's dirge drags out my heart, whets will to the whales beat
> across wastes of water . . .
>
> *– from* The Seafarer

It is noteworthy that the Nordic skalds, predecessors of the Anglo-Saxon scops, the earliest English poets, like the Celtic bards, enjoyed a quasi-magical reputation and that, as the patron of the latter was Lugh, so the former's was another solar-deity, Woden.

It is more than ubiquity or artistic merit that commends and makes Celtic mythology unique. It is more even than the fact it is a mine of information about pagan Celtic society with its love of spectacle, colour, good food, and wine. It has fundamentally shaped our ideas and ideals. For example, it was the strict rules of martial conduct by which the great heroes comported themselves that provided the basis of the medieval codes of chivalry.

Celtic society was a kind of early 'consultative democracy' in which no major decision was taken save with the consent of the assembled freemen, in practice the land-owning, warrior aristocracy. The king or *rig*, whose functions included presiding at such assemblies, was not an autocrat who made the law. The law was divinely ordained and, like Arthur, he ruled in conformity with it. Thus, Celtic kingship could, in a sense, be said to have provided the model for the principle of 'constitutional' monarchy. While the Arthurian 'Round Table,' which having neither head nor foot ensured that all who sat at it did so as equals, may have been a late interpolation, its introduction is itself informative of an attitude of mind. It first occurs in the *Roman de Brut* written by the Jerseyman Wace, possibly at the instance of Henry II (1154–89).

A sizable proportion of the knights who sailed with William of Normandy's invading forces were, in fact, not Normans, but the descendants of those very Welsh emigrés, the Bretons, as they had come to be called, expelled by the Saxons and who threw in their lot with the Conqueror in the hope of restitution. Among those who may have returned to his ancestral home, perhaps as a member of a knightly retinue, was the forefather of Geoffrey of Monmouth, author of the *Historia Regum Britanniae*. Whatever else he might have been ignorant of, Geoffrey seems to have known Brittany for, as Geoffrey Ashe points out, where he manages to make a hash of other names, he usually gets the Breton ones right.

Geoffrey's aim was to give the British what they had hitherto lacked: a history. And, having an eye to the main chance, he decided to make it one that would be acceptable and popular rather than factual, not scrupling to plagiarise other writers or simply to invent when invention might serve.

In this respect Tolstoy is quite right to see him as Britain's first best-selling author.

In the *Historia* the British monarchy is given a prestigious and classical lineage. It is traced back to Brutus, grandson of Aeneas of Troy, who, after his city's defeat by the Greeks, took refuge in Cornwall. It was from his stock that Arthur sprang, and it is the account of his life and exploits that form the culminating chapters of the work.

Though there are numerous similarities between Wace and the earlier Geoffrey, some elements, including the Round Table, do not occur in the *Historia*. Whether the Round Table came from Waces sources or was his own invention is debated, but it may well have been inserted for political reasons. Henry II, his principal patron, had usurped the throne and needed to reassure a restive nobility that he intended to rule like Arthur as first among equals.

There was another event connected with the Arthurian story which occurred, if not literally during Henry's reign, then very soon after. In 1191 monks at Glastonbury Abbey in Somerset claimed they had discovered two deeply buried bodies, those of a tall man and a slighter woman, bearing the inscription, 'HERE LIES BURIED THE RENOWNED KING ARTHUR IN THE ISLE OF AVALON, WITH GUINEVERE, HIS SECOND WIFE.' Even the wounds found on the male skeleton coincided with those which were said to have led to Arthur's death at the Battle of Camlann and the Glastonbury area is widely believed to be the site of the legendary Isle of Avalon, the place to which, according to myth, the royal corpse was borne on its funeral barge.

Plausible as this may sound, it has not silenced scepticism and it must be admitted that there is a basis for it. Part of it surrounds the queen herself and whether she could ever have existed. There is controversy about the exact meaning of her name, but the most common interpretations give 'The White Ghost' or 'The White Shadow,' hardly convincing as the name for a real person. Furthermore, a woman named Finnabair, an exact Irish counterpart for Guinevere, figures in the Cu Chulainn cycle, and she, indisputably, belongs to the Other World. This suggests that the queen may represent the vestiges of a practice common to the Celts of both Ireland and Britain – ritual marriage of the king to a territorial goddess.

Doubts such as this have led to the charge that the bones were buried and then 'discovered' by the monks themselves, who hoped thereby to attract pilgrims and contributions towards the rebuilding of their abbey seriously damaged by fire in 1184.

Strong as their motives might appear, the monks may be innocent. It has recently been shown that they actually had dug where they claimed to have done – an exercise which would surely itself have been supererogatory if the whole thing was fraudulent. What is more, their excavation took them down to a level at which there were a number of burials of the right period. And, as Geoffrey Ashe asks, why did they pick on Arthur? If it was all specious, why did they not also claim to have found the grave of the scriptural Joseph of Arimathea, also associated by legend with Glastonbury? If the abbey was, as has been claimed, a centre of religious propaganda, such a discovery would surely have been highly appropriate.

But if Arthur's Glastonbury tomb was counterfeit there was another person with a motive for perpetrating it. Apart from problems with his nobles, Henry II had others, including a threatened revolt in his Welsh domains, and the proof that the greatest of Welsh heroes was buried in England rather than Wales would be a serious blow to national morale.

Though he had died two years before the discovery of the bodies, it had been he who produced the substantive evidence of their presence and so inspired the exhumation. He had had it, he claimed, from a Welsh bard encountered during one of his whirlwind royal progresses. The question of Arthur's true burial place, as vexed a question then as now, apparently arose in conversation. His informant surprised him by telling him that it had always been known, at least to the bardic cognoscenti, that it was at Glastonbury Abbey, thereby confirming what the monks claimed to have known for centuries: that someone of great distinction – though they did not know who – was buried within its precincts. All this sounds too good to be true, and perhaps it is not entirely surprising that it has failed to silence counter-claims for the site of the royal tomb.

Two centuries later, in 1337, incited by his mother, Queen Isabella, the fifteen-year-old heir seized the crown and proclaimed himself Edward III. Once again an act of ursurpation made reassurance necessary. As part of a royal plan to revive the Arthurian knighthood Edward founded the Order of the Garter and decreed that Waces Round Table should become a physical reality. The 18-foot diameter table, decorated with representations of Arthur and twenty-four knights, that was constructed to his order was long assumed to be the original and is now to be seen at Winchester.

Nor was Edward III's the last occasion on which Arthur's name was invoked. When the Welshman Henry Tudor deposed Richard III, he was careful to christen his first born son Arthur, realising that the resonances of the name would not be lost on those he was to rule. In another symbolical gesture he had Edward III's Round Table repainted and refurbished.

Yet, for all the regularity with which he was trooped out, there is not a single contemporary document to support the belief that Arthur ever lived. Of the two greatest English historians, Bede (673–735) and the sixth-century Gildas, broadly contemporary with Arthur, the first does not mention him and the second, while describing the Battle of Mount Badon in which the Saxons were defeated by the British, omits the name of the victorious commander.

Gerald of Wales, who had been alive at the time of the Glastonbury discovery and accepted its authenticity, and hence Arthur's actuality, venerated Arthur and took Gildas as his own model. Gerald accounts for Arthur's absence from his account by reiterating a story that the historian had expunged all references to Arthur and thrown a book he had devoted to him into the sea after learning he had murdered his brother, a Scottish thane.

Loomis provides a better reason for his exclusion. Gildas was writing a homily against the abuses of his contemporaries rather than a detailed history. As he says: 'What English bishop, castigating the vices of his compatriots about 1860, would be so clumsy to allude to "The battle of Waterloo, *which was won by the Duke of Wellington*"?'

Whatever the circumstances, it is not until the appearance, in the eighth century, of the *Historia Brittonum*, traditionally ascribed to Nennius (about whom nothing is known) but more likely the compilation of a number of hands, and to the tenth-century *Annales Cambriae* that the British king is specifically mentioned.

In view of the lateness of these sources, there are some (though the argument is less popular than it once was), who believe that the writers involved were picking up local legend, thus making Arthur as fictional as Sherlock Holmes; or that, at best, the name 'Arthur' might be the alias of a pagan god: Rolleston even identified him as one named Artaius.

These doubts are not new. In the fifteenth century Caxton, publisher and printer of Malory's *Morte d'Arthur*, wrote in the preface that 'divers men hold the opinion that there was no such Arthur, and that such books as be made of him be but feigned and fables', though he later adds that 'all these things foresaid alleged, I could not well deny but that there was a noble king name Arthur and reputed one of the nine worthy, and first chief of the Christian men.'

For the Arthur-as-god hypothesis there is a scintilla of evidence In several parts of the West Country and Wales he is associated with a phantom boar-hunt, and a boar-hunt is the main subject of the earliest story in which Arthur appears – 'How Kulhwch won Olwen.' However, mythical Celtic boar-hunts predate both 'Kulhwch' and the time in which Arthur was supposed to have reigned. They may even predate the Celts themselves for a famous one occurs in the Greek Adonis myth, suggesting that the theme may once have been the common heritage of a whole group of ethnically-related peoples.

In North Wales, Rhys came across people who spoke of the 'Cwn Annwn', the hounds of Annwn (or Annwvyn), the British underworld, said to cross the paths of huntsmen. Here is an echo of the hunt which begins the story 'Pwyll, Lord of Dyfed.' Arawn, the huntsman Pwyll meets, is indeed the Lord of Annwn, though in other contexts it is Pwyll himself and later his son Pryderi who rules it. But the implication is that Arawn, Pwyll or Pryderi, and not Arthur, were the original Masters of the Hunt. Yet even this trio may have been latecomers, for the British once had another underworld ruler: Gwynn ap Nudd, who also had his phantom-hunt. These associations of the hunt with the underworld would explain why, in some of the areas where the legend survives, its leader has come to be regarded as the Devil himself.

Nonetheless, against the thesis that Arthur is simply a substitute for an earlier chthonic deity we have his character as portrayed by a host of story-tellers. If he was ever a god he must have been, not an underworld, but a solar one. As we shall see, he has many parallels with pagan heroes like the Irish Cu Chulainn, offspring of a mortal mother by the sun god Lugh, and, in the stories, stress is always laid on the festivals of spring – Easter and Pentecost – always sacred to such gods.

Though the question of Arthur's historicity will be touched on later, it is in one sense immaterial. As fictional as Sherlock Holmes he might be, but both are proofs of the durability, power, and influence of legend, for was not Sherlock Holmes responsible for a real and fundamental revolution in crime-detection?

Whether a historical Arthur existed or not, it is the mythical Arthur who is so often invoked, with his court of knights, his Round Table, and his code of chivalry, and whose influence throughout the ages has never diminished.

The presence of identifiable deities in the earliest myths attests to their sacred nature.

In other words, the stories have a kind of dual milieu of which one is the supernatural. It is a realm where mediation was the function of the Druids and, as I hope to demonstrate, there is much that is Druidic in the myths.

However, the Celtic Other World is not only that one we are so frequently offered, with its dim forests where brambles snatch at the legs, where bare-fanged creatures howl and sinister castles emerge out of the mist. To the Celts must go the credit for creating the most desirable of all paradises, Tir na n'Og, the Land of Youth, where the sunbeams fall dappled through the leaves of trees, where birds sing, and streams tinkle in an endless summer's afternoon.

The happy dweller in Tir na n'Og, lolling on its grassy knolls, bewitched by the loveliness of a companion, like Oisin with Manannan's daughter Niamh, loses all sense of passing time. Should he be so foolish as to leave, no matter how briefly, it will be to find that not years, but epochs have passed, leaving only ivy-covered ruins and skeletons.

The subjects of mythology are diverse. It tells us, for example, about the genesis of gods, the creation of the universe and our own world, and, often, how it will all end. Sometimes, though not always, it gives hints about how we must act to ensure divine goodwill. But it also treats of events, some of which go back to humanity's or the tribe's prehistory, and a rough and ready definition of much of mythology is that it is history told in other terms. A famous Greek story tells how the boy god Apollo was carried from his birthplace, the island of Delos, to the mainland on the back of a dolphin. There he scaled the sheer rocks of Mount Parnassus to the oracular shrine of the Earth Mother, slew its guardian serpent, and appropriated it to himself, naming it in honour of the obliging dolphin, Delphi. Most scholars believe that, among other things, the myth encapsulates the shift from the worship of a goddess to a god, in other words from matriarchy to patriarchy.

In the same way, the biblical myth of Abraham's proposed sacrifice of Esau and his substitution by a ram symbolises the Hebrews' turning from human to animal sacrifice, or, as Tolstoy points out, that of Jacob and Esau the nomadic pastoralism displacing the hunters.

It was the recognition of an underlying truth in mythology which sent the German archaeologist Heinrich Schliemann in search of the site of the Trojan Wars so graphically described by Homer, but previously held to be the product of literary imagination.

As we now know, our dreams contain their core of truth, too, in this case derived from events in our own, individual lives, but often mutated into symbols. So in one way myths could be called 'collective dreams.'

It is this aspect of them which is another of the ways in which they influence us for if C. G. Jung's theory of a Collective Unconscious is true, and if we each carry with us a permanently buried reservoir of material accumulated through the long march of our evolution, then it is the response of the unconscious to its echoes as found in mythology which gives to much of it its haunting quality.

To the mythology of the Celts our response is, I believe, particularly potent, at times even disturbing. Many of the incidents – such as that of the tree, ablaze on one side only, which divides a field of black from a field of white sheep, or the mysterious and sinister games in 'Enide and Gereint,' or the chalice and the bloody spear which appear to Perceval – inexplicable as they are, still seem to strike a chord in the unconscious.

So what we have in the mythology is not only a literary tour de force, not only an influential system of ideas, but also the picture of a supernatural reality, rendered in terms of symbols which, archaic as they are, live on in the Collective Unconscious.

Chapter 2

THE CELTS

Who then are the Celts, originators of this extraordinary creative achievement?

In general, they can be said to be the common ancestors of all those who call themselves 'Anglo-Saxon,' a description as accurate as if we said we were 'Anglo-Romans,' Anglo-Danes' or Anglo-Normans.' For the truth is that, despite adulteration by successive invaders, the greater proportion of the blood that courses through our veins remains Celtic, a fact which has led some English-speaking peoples, notably the Australians, to refer to themselves as 'Anglo-Celts.' Our next of kin are, accordingly, those Celts who share the British Isles with us and, among Continental nations, that other great Celtic people, the French.

Like, most other Europeans, including the Romans, Danes, and Normans, the Celts were Indo-Europeans and first emerged as a separate, identifiable people in an area round the source of the Danube about 1000 BC. Probably because of population pressure, they began to break out of their original homelands and into the surrounding areas of central Europe, then into the Iberian peninsula, northern Italy and finally into Polish Silesia, Bulgaria, Romania, Thrace, Macedonia, and even western Turkey, where they became the Galatians, recipients of one of the Pauline epistles. By the time they came to be known to the classical Mediterranean world, about the 1st millennium BC, they had become according to the Greeks, one of the three biggest 'barbarian' nations, the others being the Persians and the Scythians. The words the Greeks first used – *Keltoi kai Galatoi*, Celts and Gauls – must have been picked up from native speakers and indicate that they were what the Celts called themselves.

The last of the Greeks' 'barbarian nations,' the Scythians, were a fiercely warlike people occupying an area of what is now south-west Russia, where they were neighbours of the Celts and extremely influential upon them, a fact acknowledged, for example, in the story of 'Bricriu's Feast.' When an argument develops among the three Ulster champions Loegure, Conall, and Cu Chulainn about who is entitled to precedence, they seek the arbitration of the provincial king Cu Rui, only to find he is visiting Scythia.

It was to the Scythians that the Celts owed the male custom of growing the sweeping moustaches which so struck observers, as well as the technique of weaving wool in tartan patterns. Admirable craftsman unsurpassed in their representation of animal figures, the Scythians also passed on this skill and the Celts were to develop it along their own highly original and individualistic lines.

Another skill acquired from the same people was horsemanship and some authorities credit the Celts with introducing into Western Europe the spoked-wheel, which would have made for faster, lighter horse-drawn transport. The case is by no means conclusive, but this might account for the representation of spoked wheels on Celtic artefacts.

Like the Scythian, the Celtic territories were inhabited by a confederation of tribes, ethnically related but unable to form themselves into a coherent group, let alone a nation.

Furthermore, at some point in their history it is plain that the Celtic tribes split into two groups, the Goidels and Brythons, giving us the names Gaelic and British. They were distinguished, among other things, by the differing forms of the language, the so-called P and Q Celtic. In the former, the letters C and Q were replaced by P or B, so that, for example, the 'mac' (son) in Q-Celtic or Goidelic becomes 'ap or 'map' in P-Celtic or Brythonic, that spoken in Gaul, Wales, and what is now England.

The arrival of the Celts in the British Isles is usually set at about 800 bc, though on the evidence of grave goods which suggest a heroic society with the sort of tiered social structure reflected in the Irish myths, some authorities suggest that the brilliant Wessex Culture that appeared about 1500 bc may have been Celtic.

Territorial expansion on such a scale bespeaks a boundless dynamism. Once its tide had borne them into so much of Europe the Celts were left with a surplus that was diverted into inter-tribal warfare or collective military adventures.

In 387 bc, a Celtic force attacked and plundered Rome, demanding – and receiving – an extortionate fine as the price of withdrawal. The incident gave rise to three legendary incidents. One was the crying of the Capitoline geese whose honking warned of the invaders' approach and saved the most sacred parts of the city from desecration. The second was the Celtic commander's famous *mot*. As the ransom gold was being weighed out, a Roman dignitary complained that the weights favoured the recipients. The enemy chieftain threw his sword into the scale-pan with the comment. 'Vae, victis' (Woe to the vanquished).

The third was the actual identity of that commander himself, identified to the vanquished as 'Brennus.' A century later another force advanced on Delphi. The Delphic oracle was hurriedly consulted and declared that it would be 'saved by the white virgins.' In spite of this the treasuries of the various city-states were emptied and their contents hurried to safety. The meaning of the prophecies tends to be clear only after the events they purport to predict have occurred – a characteristic which somewhat diminishes their practical value. It was so now. The 'white virgins' were flakes of snow which began to fall prematurely and in profusion. The invaders were forced to withdraw, leaving behind the wounded of earlier encounters.

The Greek victors, curious about their attackers, discovered it was led by a man named 'Brennus.' Historians, noting the coincidence of the names in both expeditions, have concluded either that a single warrior-clan was responsible or that Brennus was the Celtic equivalent of Smith. The most recent to have been confused in this way is the German author Gerhard Herm, who even speaks of 'Brennus the elder' and 'Brennus the younger.' As we shall see in Chapter 9, there is a totally different explanation.

Continental campaigns are obliquely referred to in the myths, among them the British 'Dream of Maxen,' while those campaigns mentioned in the medieval retellings of the Arthurian stories may be echoes of them, though the possibility that such campaigns actually took place during the mid-fifth century has been given fresh impetus by the publication of Geoffrey Ashe's *The Discovery of King Arthur*.

But it was the Celtic warriors' appearance which astonished and struck terror into opponents. Their spearmen went into battle naked and with their hair, often grown to shoulder-length, matted with a lime mixture which bleached it and made it stick out in the nail-like spikes which the hair of one of the Ulster heroes was said to resemble when his battle-fury came on him. .

According to Gerald of Wales, the custom of going naked into battle survived in his own day – that is to say the mid-twelfth century. He adds that they also went unarmed, a detail found in one of the tales of the early Irish hero Cethern, while in another passage the Connaught Druid mac Roth sees a chariot being driven by a naked and unarmed man who was goading on horses and charioteer alike as if in his anxiety to reach the fray.

In battle, prisoners were rarely taken even as slaves and beheading was the fate of all who were captured. The custom was probably another borrowing from the Scythians, whom Herodotus describes as given to decapitating and scalping enemies.

The Celts, however, were more than a nation of marauding barbarians. They also had a thriving economy. Prosperity came from three sources. One was farming. Site debris shows that pig-, cattle-, sheep- and horse-rearing, were all practised. As with some African tribes, wealth was measured in head of cattle.

They were also expert agriculturists, growing cereals for domestic consumption and export. A characteristic of Celtic agriculture was the use of deep storage silos sunk into the ground and often lined with basketry. After several seasons they were usually abandoned and others dug. The old pits were then filled with earth and rubbish, providing a fruitful source for archaeologists later.

Among developments which helped increase their productivity was the plough. Although originally a bronze-working people, the Celts turned to iron-working very early and became highly skilled. Much of the forest which once covered most of southern England probably disappeared at this time as it was turned into charcoal for their furnaces. (Further substantial losses were, of course, to be caused by shipbuilding at a later period of British history.)

Besides agricultural exports, for many of the Celtic tribes there was another source of income. Strategically sited on the major trade routes, they could force merchants to pay tolls, often in kind, before moving their goods along them. In this way they were able to obtain the *objets d'art* they so admired. Among the many that have been found are the remains of an Etruscan cauldron decorated with griffins and standing on a tripod, and the lip of an ornate Rhodian flagon, while shards of Greek black-figure ware are of frequent occurrence.

Affluence also encouraged the development of native art and craftsmanship. The beauty of the scabbards, shields, helmets, and intricately inlaid swords produced for their warrior-aristocracy, as well as their mirrors, jewellery, enamelware and their magnificent torcs or neck-rings was such that the Celts have been described as the 'greatest artists north of the Alps.' The *aes dana*, which included not only artist-craftsmen, but also poets, historians, lawyers and doctors, enjoyed a status and privilege close to that of the warrior-aristocracy.

That style and taste, in both surroundings and personal adornment, were esteemed is plain particularly in the Irish Matter. We are told in the *Tain Bo Cuailnge*, The Cattle Raid of Cooley, for instance, that King Conchobhar's palace had 150 rooms panelled in red yew, while his apartment was 'guarded by screens of copper, with bars of silver and gold birds on the screens, and precious jewels in the birds' heads for eyes.'

Often the storyteller will pause in his narrative to give us a description of a character's costume. Thus when Cu Chulainn's charioteer, who was endowed with hyperacuitous vision, sees a solitary man approaching in the distance, he describes him thus:

A tall, broad, fair-seeming man. His close-cropped hair is blond and curled. A green cloak is wrapped about him, held at his breast by a bright silver brooch. He wears a knee-length tunic of kingly silk, red-embroidered in red gold, girded against his white skin.

The passage goes on to describe his black shield decorated with gold, his five-pointed spear in his hand and his forked javelin.

One does not have to look far to find similar examples and there is similar dwelling on the dress and beauties of a woman. Complexion, figure, teeth, even deportment are all described and, as to shape of face, good looks were thought to reside in one that was 'broad above, narrow below,' a form reproduced in scores of Celtic sculptures.

Though life in Celtic heathendom may well have been dominated, as some suggest, by the three Fs – feasting, fighting, and fornicating – one can discern the style and taste, as well as the sensitivity and psychological insight that lay beneath it.

Nikolai Tolstoy has given a graphic description of Celtic aristocratic life: 'Buffalo horns, magnificently ornamented, were the usual drinking receptacles, but there were glasses in plenty, as well as gold and silver goblets. Mead, wine and ale were the principal drinks . . . As in the later Medieval period, meat (beef, pork and mutton) formed the staple course of the banquet to which vegetables merely added variety. But there was fish, cheese, milk and honey and bread in abundance, and the existence of herb-gardens suggests that culinary skills were more discerning than might perhaps be expected.' He is describing the so-called Dark Ages, but there is no reason to suppose it was so very different in earlier times.

As to manners, on the whole these seem to have impressed foreign visitors. Standards of hospitality were high, strangers were fed before being asked about their business and households and occupants were strikingly clean. Ammianus Marcellinus (fourth century ad) noted approvingly 'nor in all the country . . . could any man or woman, however poor, be seen either ragged or dirty.' His comment contrasts with Caesar's statement about the depressed condition of the plebians and is further evidence that it was propaganda intended to show the benefits of Roman rule.

On the other hand, the Celtic tendency to brawling and drunkenness equally struck observers, including Plato and St. Paul. Their thirst for Greek wine was said to be such that a wine-merchant could acquire a slave-girl with a jugful or a servant for a single draught.

Again, reflections are to be found in the myths. In the hilarious 'Story of mac Datho's Pig' a quarrel breaks out between the men of Ulster and Connaught over the Champion's Portion of the roast animal. The Ulster hero Conall Cernach, having succeeded in establishing his inalienable right to it, devours not only his own share, but the entire animal, leaving the inedible foretrotters to the aggrieved Connaught men. Fighting restarts and spreads into the courtyard where, as the story-teller puts it, 'a good drinking bout broke out . . . and everyone hit someone else.'

Tolstoy compares the general picture of Celtic life with the demeanour of Scottish clan lairds such as Simon Lovat, chief of the Fraser. Distinguished for his charm, courtesy and wit at the most brilliant court in Europe, that of Louis XIV at Versailles, where he dressed in the almost effeminately ornate fashion of the age, on his hereditary estates he lived as a rough patriarch, violent in both public and private life.

The basic unit of Celtic society was the *tuath*. The word means 'people' or 'tribe', but was extended to mean the territory it occupied. At its head was the king (or *rig*), who was elected from a royal clan and was not therefore necessarily the son of a king. Though the *rig* had administrative and military functions, his most important duties were religious. These included his ritual marriage to the tutelary goddess, and upon the success of this match depended the well-being of his people and even his own survival.

In any event, the Celtic king seems to have been hedged about by restraints whose purpose, one must suppose, was to forestall despotism. For example, he had a special judge, the *brithem rig*, who was arbitrator in cases in which royal prerogatives were involved.

Within the *tuath*, the social unit was the clan or *fine*, which effectively held all land in common so that it could not be disposed of by any individual. Clan autonomy was as considerable, as it was to be in Scotland until comparatively late times.

Marriage existed in some ten different forms, though not all are known. They ranged from regular marriages to marriage by force, seduction and 'union accepted at a man's invitation'. Polygamy and concubinage were both permitted though bound by strict rules aimed at protecting both the original wife and subsequent ones.

There may be hints of one or the other in Cu Chulainn's liaison with the sidh-woman, Fand. Out of jealousy. Emer, his first wife, is on the verge of killing her rival, but is dissuaded. It is just as well, for the murder of mistress by wife was one of 'Seven Bleedings' for which harsh penalties were exacted.

Nonetheless, the lot of the Celtic woman seems to have been infinitely preferable to those in many other societies. She could inherit property, occupy positions of authority, including high military command. On marriage an equitable division of the property of both partners was arranged. In the pillow talk chapter of the *Tain Bo Cuailnge*, Queen Mebd and King Ailill discuss what each has brought to the marriage and agree their contributions have been equal.

Every individual freeman – the Celts also had slaves, though their number and effect on the economy seems to have been negligible – had an 'honour-price', an assessment of the value, usually in cattle, of his personal worth and dignity which was subject to adjustment according to the individual's own fortunes. Honour-price provided a basis for assessing compensation for grievances, but was also employed in the Celtic practice of suretyship, by which one man could act as the guarantor that another fulfilled his obligations. While his honour-price would be taken into account when judging his suitability as guarantor, he could suffer its reduction if the one for whom he had gone surety defaulted. The system is referred to in 'The Intoxication of the Ulstermen' in exchanges between Cu Chulainn and Senacha, son of Ailill, and between Fintan, son of Niall Niamglonnach and the Druid, Cathbad.

Among other unique Celtic customs were fosterage and fasting. The former, alluded to by Caesar, was the practice of sending a boy-child to live, often with other boys of the same age, away from the paternal home.

Cu Chulainn, for example. is sent to be fostered with Conall Cernach, while the fact that Arthur is described as having been fostered with Kai, later his seneschal, suggests the custom may have survived down to late times.

Fasting – strictly, 'fasting against someone' – was used as the means of securing compliance from anyone who had failed to fulfil an undertaking or against whom the faster had a grievance. (Examples of its contemporary use come readily to mind.) The theory behind its employment in pagan times was that any resulting harm would form an additional and public grievance, Furthermore, ignoring the faster could bring about a diminution of honour-price.

The Celts' inability to combine as a nation might have been less disastrous had it not been accompanied by an ungovernable aggressiveness and love of adventure.

The Romans never forgot the raid on their capital and were sharply aware that in 350 BC, less than forty years later, Celtic advances had brought them as close as Bologna. When a fresh wave of expansion began at the turn of the century the Romans decided it was time to act. After two defeats, they held the invaders at Sassoferrato and Lake Vadimon. To try to halt further incursions, Roman settlements were established along the frontiers and this maintained the peace until about the middle of the third century BC when the Celts again began to push southward. A defeat at Talamone was the beginning of a series of reverses in which Milan. Cremona, and Piacenza were taken by Roman forces.

The Celts tried to redress matters by allying themselves with the Carthaginian general Hannibal in his advance across the Alps, but when he was defeated the tribal territories in Cisalpine Gaul were picked off one by one and from about 180 bc the whole area became subject to Rome.

By the middle of the second century southern Gaul, the modern Provence, including such cities as Marseilles, Nice, and Narbonne, were also in Roman hands and the legions well placed for an advance into the rest of the country. Meanwhile, the Celts had other problems: besides pressure from the south, they were also being squeezed in the north by the advancing Germanic tribes.

Their crisis was actually exacerbated by another uniquely Celtic practice, that of *celsine* or clientism. Originally this involved only individuals, so that anyone needing protection found a patron who accorded it in return for stipulated duties, including taking up arms in his quarrels. But *celsine* had extended itself first to families, then clans, then to entire tribes. Within the context of the Celtic world the system might have worked – though it was already arousing opposition – but on occasion a tribe would seek protection from a non-Celtic people. The client/patron relationship was then all too liable to become one of total subservience to the stronger partner.

When the Aedui placed themselves under Roman clientship in a quarrel with the Arverni and Allobroges, Roman occupation of the two tribal territories had placed them in control of the routes between the Rhone, Saone and Loire rivers. It was not an advantage they were inclined to relinquish. By the first century Julius Caesar was in a position to subdue the Helvetii in what is now Switzerland, as well as suppress the rebellion of the young Arvernian leader, Vercingetorix, thereby bringing all Gaul under his rule. He also launched two sorties against Britain.

In spite of these incursions, for the time being Britain was spared occupation. Then, in AD 43, it was invaded by Claudius. In a short time, the domain of the principal Celtic king Cunobelinus (Shakespeare's Cymbeline) submitted and his capital Camulodunum (Colchester) made that of a Roman province.

The Roman seizure of Britain is yet another example of how *celsine* with a non-Celtic people could go awry. In this case, Cartimandua, queen of the large northern British tribe of Brigantes, placed herself under Roman protection. When Caratacus, leader of an unsuccessful anti-Roman rebellion, fled to Brigantia she had him arrested, placing the occupiers sufficiently in her debt for them to come to her aid when her consort and co-ruler, Venutius, rebelled against her pro-Roman policies. Although king and queen were temporarily reconciled, she finally left him for the royal armour-bearer, Vellocatus. Venutius gave chase with his troops and again the Romans rescued her. But her people were to pay a high price: in AD 71, Brigantia was annexed.

With the conquest of Britain the Celts had been nullified as a military threat, though their lands were not completely occupied. In Britain the zone of occupation ended at Hadrian's Wall and Ireland was never entered at all.

For our knowledge of the history of these areas we are dependent wholly upon myth and the nuggets of fact which undoubtedly underlie it have yet to be panned out. The task is not made any easier by the Celtic habit of recording events not as they actually occurred but as they would have liked them to. This is done less to portray themselves in an unfailingly heroic light than in one that was artistically satisfying – a characteristic not entirely missing in the Celtic character even today.

Even if not total, the Romans' hold was sufficient for them to begin the task of consolidation. One of their first actions to this end was to extirpate

Druidism, the excuse being their desire to rid the unfortunate British, as they had done for the Gauls, of a superstition which included cruel and bloody sacrifice.

At the same time, it has to be recognised that Celtic religion was very different from Roman. The latter was so totally secularised that the interests of the gods and those of the state invariably coincided. Some Caesars became gods after death; some, like Gaius Julius, in their lifetime. By contrast, among the Celts every decision in life was referred to the arbitration of the gods, via the Druids.

In any event, in AD 61 a shock detachment under Suetonius seised Mon (Anglesey). An uncharacteristically purple passage by Tacitus describes how the legionaries crossing the Menai Straits in the early morning light were confronted on the far shore by a 'dense array of armed warriors' with women in black dashing among the ranks 'like the Furies,' hair dishevelled and waving brands, while the Druids with uplifted hands called down 'dreadful imprecations.' It was a sight before which the bravest might quail, but the day, like so many others, was the Romans'. The Druids were consigned to the sacrificial fires they had themselves prepared for the defeated and in the ensuing days the occupiers axes rang harshly against the trees of the sacred groves.

How great was the defeat was graphically demonstrated centuries later. Clearance work for the building of a Second World War airfield at Llyn Cerrig Bach, formerly a lake in Anglesey, uncovered a treasure trove which included slave chains and even complete chariots, as well as many other objects from all over Britain thrown into the water in a vain attempt to invoke the aid of the gods against the invaders.

Throughout the subsequent four hundred years of occupation, Druidism was proscribed in Britain as elsewhere, though even under this constraint it almost certainly survived in the remoter areas and in secrecy, evidence for which is not only the survival of the myths themselves, but also the markedly Druidic strain to be detected within them.

Chapter 3

THE BARDS

According to the classical writers, three classes enjoyed particular esteem in Celtic society. Heading the list were Druids, but after them came those whom they call the Vates and the Bards. The first – the source of our word 'vaticination' – were, so they tell us, diviners, *faithi* in Irish. The second, the Irish *filid*, were poets, musicians, and story-tellers; in other words, custodians of mythology.

However, this information is already of comparatively late date, for it was only when the Celts reached the Mediterranean littoral about the middle of the first millennium BC that the classical world's acquaintanceship with them began. By this time their society had undergone considerable change and it is plain that in earlier times the Druidic functions had included those later taken over by the Vates and Bards, and that, furthermore, the separation was never absolute. This is one reason why, in the Irish stories, the terms 'bard' and 'Druid' are so often interchangeable and those described by one word when first introduced will be called by the second in a subsequent passage. Thus, we are told in the *Tain Bo Cuailnge* that the 'sweet-mouth harpers of Cain Bile' were also 'Druids of great knowledge.' Even after separation had taken place, the bards retained, as Markale says, something of the character of priests, seeing themselves 'as one of the founts of wisdom in the Celtic world.'

It is significant that the British bards adopted the custom of putting the title 'ollave,' originally reserved for Druids and roughly equivalent to our own 'doctor,' but with evocations of the word 'father,' before their names. According to Graves, it was still in use among Welsh bards up till the time of the Cromwellian conquest.

Exactly how a man became a bard is not known, though *The Triads of the Island of Britain,* an anthology of triplets in which each subject is introduced in a single line followed by three examples, suggests that in some cases the calling might have been hereditary, for No. 40 tells us that three bards, Tristvardd, Dygunnelw, the Bard of Owein, and Avan Verddig, bard of Cadwallon, were the 'sons of bards.'

Indicative of a Druidic past was both the enormous prestige and reward the bards enjoyed. This is comparable only with that of a modern rock singer and, in some ways, is greater. From one of his patrons the Welsh bard Taliessin received a hundred racehorses, a hundred purple cloaks, a hundred bracelets, fifty brooches, and a fine sword.

Although we should remember that it is the bards themselves who are telling us these things, and that it would have been to their advantage to stress, if not exaggerate, the generosity of past patrons to encourage present ones, there is no doubt a core of truth. By tradition, no gift could be refused to a bard even by a king and there are several examples of full and unscrupulous use of being made of this.

At the same time we have instances of mythological characters who impersonated bards solely to obtain a desired object. In one of the British tales, the magician Gwydion, who covets the swine belonging to Pryderi, king of Dyfed, resorts to just such a device. Having gained entrance to the court through it, he demands the swine in payment for his stories. Pryderi refuses on the ground that he has promised his subjects he will not part with them by way of gift or sale. Gwydion suggests a compromise: the letter of the agreement does not specifically forbid exchange and he magically produces twelve magnificently caparisoned horses and twelve hounds with which he temps Pryderi. The king accepts. But he has been duped, for the chimerical creatures dissolve within twenty-four hours, by which time Gwydion and his companions have made good their escape. Pryderi got off comparatively lightly: it was said that a king was forced to sacrifice an eye at the behest of a heartless bard.

In at least some cases, bards seem to have been free to cross the tribal frontiers – a privilege also accorded to the Druids – and like them were apparently exempt from military service. In some ways they were almost outside the tribe itself, for whenever there was an intertribal war, the bards of both sides jointly withdrew to some suitable vantage point and there observed the ensuing struggle, assessing the merits of the principal warriors, rather as cricket commentators covering a Test Match for their respective countries will pool their opinions of batsmen. The analogy is not a flippant one, for the sense of a game, played according to a set of rules, is predominant in descriptions of Celtic warfare.

For all this, we should not assume that the bard was an uncommitted observer of the life of his society. According to the Triads, it was bards who 'committed the three beneficial assassinations of the Isle of Britain,' in fact giant-slayings, and Triad No. 91 lists 'the three beneficial artisans of the Isle of Britain,' also bards. They are: Corvinwr, who gave the Cambrians their first ship with sails and a rudder; Morddal, who taught the use of stone and lime – in the words of the Triad, 'at the time the emperor Alexander was subduing the world'; and Coel, son of Cyllin who made the first mill wheel.

But these activities, useful as they might be, were secondary to their main one: that of providing music and story. This was so deeply woven into the fabric of Celtic life that bards are found even in households of the gods.

The Dagda, sire of a whole generation of deities, has his harper and personal harp. Stolen, it flies back to the hands of its true owner when he addresses it with the invocation 'Come, apple-sweet murmurer. Come, four-angled frame of harmony. Come, Summer. Come, Winter, from the mouths of harps and bags and pipes.'

Thus Irish bardism, at any rate, seems to have a divine origin. Of the craft in Britain we are told in Triad No. 92 that the three inventors of song and record were Gwyddon Ganhedon, Hu the Mighty, and Tydain, 'who first conferred art on poetic song and made it the medium of record.'

The names of illustrious bards have come down to us, and some of them, like the Irish Tuan mac Cairill and Amergin and the Welsh Taliessin and Aneirin, are possibly historical figures. The magician known to Arthurian legend as 'Merlin' may well have been based partly on a bard named Myrddin. (The question of Merlin and his identity is the subject of Nikolai Tolstoy's admirable book, *The Quest for Merlin*.)

Some believe Merlin's name to be commemorated in the place-name Carmarthen, or 'Myrddin's caer,' and it is true that the suffix '-caer,' a stronghold, is often attached to a personal name, as in Caerleon. However, modern scholarship suggests that rather than the town being named after Myrddin, his name was derived from the town. 'Myrddin' is the Welsh form of the P-Celtic *Moridunon*. 'Mor' means 'the sea' and Dunn, present in names like Dundee in Scotland and Loudun in France, means a fort, yielding a 'Sea-fort.'

The bard was expected to be trained in specific skills, both narrative and musical. The latter included command of the three Noble Harp Strains: the Lament Strain, which could bring his hearers to tears; the Laughter Strain, which replaced tears of sorrow for those of joy; and the Sleep Strain, which could lull them to slumber. Among those who were masters of the three Noble Strains was the solar-deity Lugh, surnamed 'Lugh of the Many Skills' on account of his wide-ranging versatility, of which bardic skill was but one.

Besides the Noble Strains, there is evidence that the Celts, like the ancient Egyptians and the Indians today, had particular musical modes assigned to certain seasons, which may explain the 'Come Summer, come Winter' references in the Dagda's invocation to his purloined harp. Like the Indian *ragas,* too, it is possible that there were modes for particular times of day.

Music could not merely soothe the savage breast; apparently it could also still it permanently, for we are told in the 'Tain Bo Froech' that when Froech's hornplayers preceded him into his court, their melody was such that thirty of his guests 'died of yearning.' On the other hand, it had its curative aspect, too, as in the story of the dumb prince Maon, whose speech was restored by the melody of a master-harper.

Though the Celtic love for song and story amounted to an addiction, it was not solely on this account that the bard enjoyed honour and reward. He also possessed magical powers.

Seized by what the Welsh still call *awen*, the divine muse, he did not merely declaim, he prophesied. As late as the times of Gerald of Wales individuals known collectively as *awenyddion* were to be found and were consulted by those who wished to know the future. In order to discover it they threw themselves into frenzied paroxysms, babbling incoherently and giving all the indications of being entranced. It was for the questioner to winnow his answer from the chaff. Gerald, though he does not seem to have witnessed the performance, suggest the *awenyddion* may have been in the thrall of demons or spirits – a not untypical medieval conclusion. He casts doubt on the validity of the answers given in this way on the ground that if the same question were put twice it received different responses each time. All the same, one cannot help being reminded of the frenzies of the Delphic Pythia in their prophetic trance

Even more dreaded was another of the bard's quasi-magical skills: the power to sing the *glam dicin*. This was a form of lampoon with the potency of a spell which at one extreme could be used to drive out rats and at the other to disable, even kill, a human victim.

The *glam* was feared as much as or more than the weapons of an enemy, and even the greatest heroes avoided falling victim to it. When Ferdia is ordered by Mebd, his queen, to do mortal combat with his fellow student-in-arms, Cu Chulainn, he tries to refuse only to be warned he will be satirised. He does the queen's bidding and dies for his efforts. It is a similar threat which compels Cu Chulainn himself to yield his three spears to the enemy bards who ask for them. By gaining them they are able to master and so destroy him.

As with so much else in Celtic life, the *glam* shares a mythical origin. When the divine Irish bard Coirpre visits the Fomorian tyrant Bress, offended by his shabby treatment, he leaves the palace without taking leave of his host and instead of the customary panegyric sings the first *glam* uttered in Ireland:

No meat on plates,
No milk from kine;
No welcome for the late;
No reward for bards:
May Bress's cheer be what he gives to others!

The Fomorian king came out in red blotches and, since a monarch must be unblemished, had no option but to abdicate. Later, when the Fomorians made war on their enemies, the Tuatha De Danann, Coirpre, himself a member of the divine Tuathan clan, again put his satirical skill to use to 'take away' the honour of the Fomorian warriors, thereby incapacitating them even before the battle.

Like *awen*, belief in the power of the bard's lampoon continued in Wales well into the Middle Ages, and it was believed that it could bring its victim out in blisters. In the light of our modern knowledge of the intimate relationship between psyche and soma, mind and body, it seems far from inconceivable.

No one who has travelled in the Celtic lands can fail to recognise that the predilection for story, poetry, and music is not a thing of the past. In Wales, there is the *eisteddfod* whose beginnings go back at least to the fifteenth century, though three hundred years earlier Gerald was praising the ingenuity and inventiveness of his native poets, especially in their own tongue. Among literary devices he singles out alliteration, a device also used by the Old English scops.

The high point of the *eisteddfod* is the *gorsedd*, the assembly of poets, at which the bardic crown is awarded. A similar, though less renowned event, takes place in Cornwall and the migration of large numbers of Welsh emigrants to the United States, and particularly to Ohio, led to its establishment there.

Music in the forms both of singing and the playing of instruments, especially the harp, is another central feature of Celtic life that shows a remarkable continuity. Outsiders, visiting chapels or any of those other places at which the Welsh foregather, are constantly amazed, not simply by their readiness to burst into song, but by their capacity for spontaneous counterpoint and harmonisation. This characteristic was another of those which elicited delighted comment from the deeply patriotic Gerald of Wales, who says of his fellow countrymen that when a choir gathered to sing 'you will hear as many parts as there are performers, all joining together in the end to produce a single organic harmony.'

Gerald also describes how guests, arriving in a Welsh household, will be entertained by the daughters of the family on the harp. It was plainly not regarded as a uniquely feminine accomplishment for a few lines later he declares that 'the menfolk consider playing on the harp to be the greatest of all accomplishments.' He also tells us that besides the harp, they played two other instruments, the pipe and the *crwth* or crotta, a bowed instrument with affinities to the fiddle. The harp and fiddle are still intrinsic to Irish music. Gerald describes the Irish as playing their instruments at great speed and expresses admiration for their ability to maintain musical balance while moving their fingers so quickly, a talent they have also retained.

From early times the bard must have been a member of a professional body with its own discipline tradition, and restrictions on membership.

Triad No. 58 says that what it calls 'the three primary bards of Britain,' Plennydd, Alawn, and Gwron, established a system of licensing and of custom and privilege for bards, while before their time no privilege existed 'other than that which was obtained through kindness and civility.' In other words Plennydd, Alawn, and Gwron put on an institutional basis what had previously been more or less an *ad hoc* arrangement. However, if the bards were descended from the Druids it seems unlikely that there was ever a time when they were not organised, since they give an impression of close-knit organisation almost unique in the Celtic world.

In keeping with their professional status, the bards underwent a rigorous training. In many ways this parallels the twenty-year Druidic novitiate spent largely, so Caesar tells us, in learning countless verses. For the Druids these would have included far more than the epic and myth which formed the bard's repertoire. Rhyme and alliteration originated as *aides-mémoire,* the entirety of Druidic lore was transmitted orally and also included an entire and highly complex system of law and precedent.[1]

If, after the split with Druidism proper, the bard was at least spared this, the amount of material that had to be committed to memory was still formidable. Jeffrey Gantz's belief that the storyteller did not memorise the entire story, only its outlines, is not supported by other evidence, which suggests that the apprentice-bard was expected to memorise his teacher's words down to the last epithet, figure of speech, and turn of phrase. When qualified he undoubtedly added touches of his own, but even these would have been within the strict rules governing composition.

A hint of what was expected is to be found in the last paragraph of the 'Dream of Rhonabwy' whose writer informs us that 'neither bard nor storyteller knows the Dream without a book, because of the many colours of the horses and the variety and strange colours of armour and equipment and precious mantles and powerful stones.' This makes it sound as if bards and storytellers were not normally expected to use such aids.

In Ireland the *fili* seems to have continued the recitation of the traditional stories even after the country's conversion to Christianity, with only a cursory genuflection in the direction of the new altar. But in Britain things followed a totally different course, first because of the Roman proscription of Druidism, and secondly because of the country's entirely different socio-political structure: that of a Roman province. Though we know that something of the old faith survived in the remoter areas and in secrecy, the British ruling class had been substantially Romanised, largely through the policy of rewarding 'friends of Rome' with titles and the

---

1 The Celtic tradition of oral law, harking back to Druidic practice, was maintained in the Isle of Man until recent times with its so called Breast Law which had precedence over the written. A similar system was found among the Irish *Brehons* until their extirpation by the English in Elizabethan times.

opportunities of enrichment. An example can be seen at Fishbourne near Chichester in West Sussex. Here the local client-king, Cogidubnus, thanks to the favour of the occupiers, was able to build up such a fortune that his palace, whose remains can be seen, was one worthy of the Imperial City itself. There is very little doubt that among the pre-conquest nobility men like Cogidubnus were regarded as little more than upstarts.

The result of these policies was that, just as the Celts dwelling near the Greek trading-post of Massilia in southern France were said to be 'more Greek than the Greeks,' the British were, in many respects, more Roman than the Romans. The barbaric past, symbolised by Druidism and its mythology, had, of course, been the principal target of a sustained propaganda attack, the success of which can be gauged even in our own times. In defiance of contemporary knowledge of Celtic society and its achievements, history books persist in conveying the impression that before the coming of the Romans the British languished in a Dark Age. This merely echoes the attitudes of the Briton of the fourth and fifth centuries AD, who was less interested in stories from his rude and distant past than in the polished and sophisticated literature of the classical mediterranean civilisation which had been the occupiers' gift to him.

Even in the latter days of occupation, when Christianity began to spread among the legions and native populace, its form and style remained essentially and no doubt comfortingly Roman. The priest spoke Latin, wore the clothes of a Roman gentleman, and, insofar as churches existed, they were Romanesque in style. In any case, there was probably a stronger feeling of participation in the religious revolution in Britain than elsewhere, for Constantine, the first Christian emperor, had actually acceded to the purple while stationed as an officer in the country.

Nikolai Tolstoy presents what I believe to be a fundamentally correct picture of the British intelligentsia of the time. The sixth-century Gildas, himself a Briton but writing in the conqueror's Latin, in his *De excidio et Conquestu Britanniae*, uses the word *cives*, citizens, to describe his countrymen, as if he takes for granted that they share in St. Paul's privilege of 'Roman citizenship,' and, at the same time, lays savagely about at what are obviously bards employed by King Maelgwn of Gwynedd in North Wales, who, as we shall see later, was probably helping to conserve and disseminate the Matter from a past vernacular tradition.

If the survival of even the shreds of that tradition was now an even greater embarrassment than it had been in the times of Roman paganism, its tenacity was soon recognised. Unable to suppress it, efforts were to purge and make it fit reading for the devout, and the bard, brought under the wing of a largely ecclesiastical officialdom, was expected to confine himself to uplifting subjects. Invention was limited to the stylistic, which gradually petrified into a set of conventions that lead to complete creative stultification.

In so far as mythological allusion was employed it was always in substantially Christianised form and, if necessary, the subject matter was hammered and twisted into the required shape. Two examples that spring to mind are the Grail story and the liaison of Lancelot and Guinevere, or, for that matter, of Tristan and Isolt. In each case pagan themes have been substantially modified and new material added to make them fit the environment of the new religion.

With the Grail episode it is even possible to observe the steps in a progressive transmutation from the pagan. In the earliest version in our possession, what the hero sees at the castle of the Fisher King is a severed head on a platter; as we have seen, decapitation was a Celtic custom, which suggests that the episode is a relic of the practice. In later versions platter and gory contents become the chalice from which Jesus celebrated the first communion and which, by a series of coincidences, has turned up in Britain. In the cases of Lancelot's and Tristan's liaisons with their queens, a knowledge of Celtic paganism gives us a clue to what lies behind what to Christian eyes was damnable adultery.

However, long before Christianisation had been completed, the Saxon invasion forced much of British aristocracy to leave their native land for Brittany. With the humiliation of being turned into refugees on top of military defeat, it was hardly surprising that they should have given precedence to the recollection of former glories made more splendid at each retelling. Insofar as an earlier literature was recalled at all, it was as stories in which Arthur and his paladins had supplanted earlier, pagan figures.

How then did the pagan mythology survive at all? Robert Graves believed it was due to the efforts of what might be called a 'bardic splinter group' which broke away from the officially sponsored one, though more probably they had never been members of it.

How rigorously the Roman prohibition on Druidism was enforced we do not know, but as soon as it came into existence the Druids would certainly have taken measures to circumvent it and sustain belief. In my opinion, one subterfuge they employed was to return to a former role: taking up the harp once more, they passed themselves off as bards who, we know, continued their activities throughout the Roman era. Thus they would have been in much the same position as the Catholic priests of Elizabethan times who, passing themselves off as artisans, were able to sustain and encourage those who cleaved to the Old Faith. Though hard proof is non-existent, there are indicators: for example, the fact that late Welsh folklore credits bards with the Druidic powers of divination and trance.

Unlike the official bards, the patrons of these Druids-in-disguise were not the Romanised upper classes, secular or ecclesiastic, but remained the Old Faithful who, besides the dwellers in rural cottage and farmstead, included certain elements of the nobility, among them perhaps the King Maelgwn against whom Gildas railed.

However, in Britain, throughout the Roman occupation and afterwards, a linguistic revolution had been taking place. The old Brythonic or P-Celtic was evolving into Welsh. It is in enclaves of conservatism that old forms of language, despised as primitive and rustic in more fashion-conscious circles, are preserved. Many examples are available, but typical is the French *patois* spoken in the Channel Islands. Once universal, in more recent times it has become the exclusive vernacular of the countryman, unknown and ridiculed in the upper reaches of the islands' society.

Emigrés, too, conserve language. Metropolitan Germans used to mock the archaism of the language spoken in the Baltic communities, and American English still retains many elements of that spoken at the time of Pilgrim Fathers.[2]

The language of the unofficial bards must have been something which those Breton knights in the Conqueror's expeditionary force found congenial and familiar. Long disdained, after the Norman Conquest the rebel bards would no doubt have found themselves once more attached to the households of wealthy and influential men. However, as far as the matter of the stories is concerned it must have undergone yet more change at this time as material of indisputably French provenance began and continued to penetrate the Welsh.

Meanwhile, in France itself the Breton Arthurian heritage was to be changed in ways which were even more fundamental. From early times, the Christian Church had been concerned at the lack of a feminine element in the heavenly hierarchy. This was rectified by the exaltation of Christ's mother, round whom a whole body of attributes, mostly without scriptural sanction, were woven. This special kind of idealisation of womanhood as represented by the Virgin Mary – it was also, as feminists have pointed out, an enslavement – generated with it the romantic tradition and, in its wake, the *amour courtoise*. Aspects of this, inherent in Celticism, had been expressed in the myths, but by judicious changes of emphasis they became stories totally pleasing to the new taste.

In fact, the result was to produce an image of woman which, while celebrating her beauty or merit, as the earlier myths had done, diminished her corporeal reality. Gone is the old camaraderie, such as that of Cu Chulainn and Emer. Gone, too, is the old Rabelaisian earthiness. Instead of 'the friendship of the thighs,' such favours as the gowned and wimpled ladies of

---

2 Examples are, the American exclamation, 'Swell!,' almost certainly from the Puritan, "Tis well!' and the short u-sound of American where British English has a short o-sound, as in 'honesty' which Americans pronounce 'unnesty,' using the same sound as we use in 'love' and 'month.'

the *amour courtois* grant are likely to be limited to a scarf to be worn from a tilt-helm (many were fitted with hooks for the purpose).

A single example illustrates the change that took place. At the height of a battle Queen Mebd is overcome by the need to relieve herself and asks her champion Fergus to make a shelter of shields that she may do so. 'My God,' he tells her, 'you've picked a fine time.'

'I can't help it. I'll die if I don't.'

One cannot help feeling that the medieval Arthurian heroine faced with such a situation would actually have been expected to choose death.

— PART II —

THE CONTENT OF THE MYTHS

Chapter 4

THE SURVIVING VERSIONS
AND THEIR SOURCES

Despite the size of the Celtic cultural province at its peak, it is only in the British Isles that a substantial body of mythology has survived. All that can be found in Continental Europe, apart from the Arthurian material whose importation in post-Roman times via the Bretons has been discussed, are a few folk-tales with motifs suggesting Celtic mediation. But of what must originally have been a large body of matter, including written documents, virtually nothing remains.

One reason for this was the French government's ban, in force until recent times, on the use of the Breton tongue, effectively erasing whatever literature may previously have existed in it, save what had been translated into French or was preserved as verbally transmitted folk legend. Among frequent motifs is the underwater city and its bewitching women inhabitants who constantly tempt earth-dwellers to join them in it, a typically Celtic theme hinting at the age and provenance of the material.

However, despite surviving, what we have in the British Isles is not only greatly changed, but riddled with omissions. As well as the friction of time, there are obvious reasons for the degeneration. The pagan Celtic was an oral literature and, despite the apparent care taken by storytellers in preserving their material, was subject to change as it was passed from one to another. In any case, as entertainers in the strictest sense, storytellers would have succumbed to the temptation to embellish, adding touches and perhaps entire incidents popular with their listeners, which helped to obscure the primitive elements in their material.

In both Britain and Ireland, those who first gave the stories written form were monks and they could have been pardoned for feeling antipathy toward these blatantly heathen tales. As we saw in the last chapter, in Britain they faced more than ecclesiastical disapproval. There was also the disdain of the educated for what they had been fully persuaded was the barbaric past. And though those whom we described as unofficial bards might have been untouched, by the early Middle Ages, even they seem to have lost the sense that their texts were sacred or had, at any rate, forgotten their underlying meaning. This is something to which we shall return, for, perhaps paradoxically, the British Matter contains more relics of Druidism than the Irish.

Ireland, on the other hand, had been spared Roman occupation and so had had less exposure to Europe and its classics. The *filid*, unlike the bards, were under no cultural pressure to emulate allegedly superior classical models. At the same time, Irish social and administrative structures having remained largely unchanged, the milieux of their stories, however archaic their origins, remained largely familiar to the hearers. It is for both these reasons that we find in the Matter of Ireland references to Druids.

Surprisingly, there is little sign that the Irish missionaries, when they came in contact with it, were shocked by what they found. Recording the story from the mouth of a bard, the redactor might append the rider that he had taken it down as relayed, but personally did not believe a word of it. Sometimes he simply ended with the words 'Finit – Amen.' There seems to have been little attempt at censorship, though in a few cases the tale ends with the hero's baptism and, if he is known to have died long before the conversion, he might be miraculously reincarnated in order to undergo it. Even the lack of sexual inhibition so often manifested was reproduced unaltered and without overt disapproval.

Besides the different cultural climates of the two islands there were other factors which brought this about. Dillon supposes that the wide gulf separating the Irish mythology from anything suggesting the 'scripture of a religious cult, may have been one reason why the Irish monks felt able to help conserve it. It was simply a fund of good stories, or the history of events that had occurred before their own arrival. They embarked on the task of recording it with the same land of conscientiousness as tenth-century Scandinavian Christians like Snorri Storluson – himself a priest – recorded the myths of the Nordic paganism.

Another, and more important, reason why the Irish missionaries failed to react with horror to what they found must have been their day-to-day familiarity with pagan neighbours. No doubt, before being dispatched, they would have been as thoroughly indoctrinated about the excesses of heathendom as those who came to Britain. But stories of atrocities would have begun to pale once they began to mingle with the alleged perpetrators. What they then saw were not people preoccupied mainly with slaughter, rape, and pillage, but with the familiar concerns of living – people, what is more, whose qualities of character, such as their enormous respect for truth, they quickly began to admire and find consistent with their own teachings.

It was hard, in these circumstances, to feel the same hostility towards the past as was felt by men like Gildas in Britain who had had no personal experience of what it can have been like. St. Patrick and St. Columba may have met Druids; it is unlikely Gildas knew them other than from the pages of Lucan and Tacitus.

However, none of this should blind us to the fact that admiration and, in some cases, patriotism may have led the Irish copyists to omit incidents they found too grossly at odds with the principles of the new religion. Besides, as Gantz points out, one has to allow for the fact they were not literary men capable of understanding the nuances of those who were.

The truth is that, taking as a whole the versions of the mythology in our possession, one is bound to agree with what Matthew Arnold said specifically about the Welsh: that it was evident that the re-teller of the stories was 'pillaging an antiquity of which he does not fully possess the secret: he is like a peasant building his hut on the site of Helicarnassus or Ephesus; he builds, but what he builds is full of materials of which he knows not the history, or knows by a glimmering tradition merely.'

They were also human and must have wearied of the very considerable effort of transcribing, word by word, material conveyed orally and often taking so long in the telling as to occupy several nights.

To confuse the issue further, long before the stories first came to be written down, the tellers had begun interpolating alien material. That the British borrowed extensively from the Irish is well exemplified in the story of 'Kulhwch and Olwen.' Among Arthur's enormous band of courtiers are listed 'Cynchwr ap Nes,' plainly Conchobhar mac Nessa, the Ulster king; 'Cubert ap Daere,' who is Cu Rui mac Daere; 'Fercos ap Poch,' Fergus mac Roech; and 'Corvil Bervach,' who is plainly Conall Cernach. In the same tale Sgilti Lightfoot, who can run along the tops of trees, has been shown to be Caoilte, the Irish possessor of a similar useful talent. Loomis has demonstrated that 'Tristan and Isolt' was probably based on the Irish 'Grainme and Diarmait' and a homologue for the horse-eared King Mark is found in the Irish King Labraidh Lorc.

Nor is this understandable cross-fertilisation between two neighbouring Celtic peoples the limit to the exchange. Some scholars have identified the magician Gwydion of the Welsh stories with the Norse Odin. The equation is dubious, but Gwydion's coupling with Lleu (the British form of Lugh), whom Odin strongly resembles, and the unscrupulous trickery the former often resorts to – such as in his effort to acquire Pryderi's swine or to persuade Lleu's mother to name and arm him – is totally consistent with the character of the Nordic god who was sometimes called 'the Great Deceiver.' As Woden, Odin was introduced into Britain by the Saxons, and 'Gwydion' would be an appropriate Welsh transliteration. Later, when the French troubadours had started to use the Celtic material there were borrowings back so that characters with French names begin to appear.

But cross-fertilisation, considerable as it may have been, cannot explain all the parallels to be found in the two Matters, for in some cases the same creatures or events appear in both, but in different contexts. For example, there is the salmon. The Irish Finn acquires wisdom by eating one of the 'salmon of wisdom' that inhabit Fec's Pool in the River Boyne. In the British Matter, Kai and the magician Gwyrhyr also encounter a salmon of wisdom, this time living in the Severn. Instead of eating it they use it as a means of transport, being carried on its shoulders to Mabon ap Modron's prison, the location of which the fish alone knows.[3] The conclusion must be that the concept of 'wise' salmon is one going back in Celtic belief to the time before the separation of Goidels and Brythons.

The division of the myth canon into the Matter of Ireland and the Matter of Britain reflects a separation that was linguistic as well as geographical. Of the two, the Irish, by far the greater in quantity, began to achieve written form in the centuries immediately following the conversion of the country in the fourth century, but regrettably, with so much else, these earliest and most reliable recensions are long since lost. All we now possess are copies of copies. Even the oldest literary record, a poem by the bard Amergin, dates back only to the seventh century AD.

Among reasons for the lacuna were the activities of Scandinavian raiders who destroyed all whose value as booty was not immediately obvious. The material so lost includes the early eighth-century *Book of Druimm Snechtai*. From the list of contents which has survived we know that among the material in it was 'The Wooing of Etain,' 'The Destruction of Da Derga's Hostel,' and 'The Birth of Cu Chulainn,' now available to us only in later versions.

Among the surviving Irish documents one of the earliest is the *Book of the Dun Cow (Lebor na hUidre)*, which gets its name from the fact that the original was said to have been written on the hide of a favourite cow belonging to the seventh-century St. Ciaran. The extant volume is fragmentary, but contains the name of its scribe, Maelmuiri, known to have been martyred by the Vikings in the cathedral of Clocmacnois in 1106. Despite its dilapidation it contains virtually complete versions of 'The Destruction of Da Derga's Hostel,' 'The Birth of Cu Chulainn,' and 'Bricriu's Feast,' together with incomplete versions of the 'Wooing of Etain,' 'The Intoxication of the Ulstermen,' and the *Tain Bo Cuailnge*.

Another early document is the *Dindsenchas* or *The History of Places* (the word actually means topography, and especially that of famous places), a collection of Old Irish legends, each set against the backdrop of a particular site, and existing in both prose and metrical forms. It is contained in a manuscript at Rennes in Brittany and at the Bodleian Library at Oxford, as well as in the *Book of Leinster (Lebor Laigen)*, dated 1150, carrying the signature of Finn mac Gorman, Bishop of Kildare.

The same volume also contains an account of the mythical invasions of Ireland, the *Tain Bo Cuailnge*, 'The Exile of the Sons of Usnech,' the 'Melodies of Buchet's House,' 'The Destruction of Dinn Rig,' as well as

---

3 It is interesting, in this context, that Victorian children used to be encouraged to eat fish because it 'improved the brain.' Salmon was supposed to be specially efficacious.

other material. It is dated to the twelfth century, but, in view of the archaic nature of some of its contents, may be as early as the sixth century. For example, it mentions the existence of an idol called Cromm Cruaich on the plain of Mag Sleacht to which children were annually sacrificed at Samain. Another story describes the massacre of fifty captives taken in battle by King Eochu Muigmedon, a historical figure believed to have reigned over Leinster from 358 to 366.

Much later, but bound into the same collection, is the Yellow Book of Lecan and a manuscript designated Egerton 1792. The Yellow Book itself, though it contains full versions of the 'Wooing of Etain' and The Death of Aife's Only Son,' as well as the 'Fate of the Children of Tuirenn,' mentioned in the ninth-century Cormac's Glossary, dates only to the fourteenth century, while Egerton, which has 'The Dream of Oengus,' is actually dated 1419. An account of The Second Battle of Mag Tuireadh, thought by many to be a late invention, is contained in Harleian MS 5280.

Probably because until about the sixteenth century the language and literature of Scotland and Ireland were one and the same, we have little in written form coming from the first, though traditional stories were being told at least down to the nineteenth century. A number of clerics deplored the Highlanders' preference for legends of the Tuatha De Danann, the divine clan known from the Irish Matter, over the more uplifting scriptural stories. In many known instances, ecclesiastical disapproval was circumvented by replacing the anathematised pagan gods with Christian saints. Thus, St. Michael plays exactly the same role in some of them as the popular Tuathan Lugh in the Irish canon. Professor Anne Ross found many of these stories still being told in rural areas, though as the generation which knew them dies out so, too, will they.

Apart from this oral folk literature there are some Scottish transition stories, that is to say those in which the supercession of paganism by Christianity is portrayed. The oldest collection of these is in a manuscript called The Dean of Lismore's Book, named after its compiler, James MacGregor, the dean of Lismore in Argyllshire, who some time before the year 1518 gathered under one head all the traditional poetry he could lay his hands on.

In Ireland the transition period is represented, among other examples, by the thirteeth-century Acallam na Senorec (Colloquy of the Elders), an anthology of stories which continue the legends of Oisin (Ossian) mac Finn and his band of warriors down to Christian times.

The British Matter is contained in what have come to be called The Four Ancient Books of Wales, The Black Book of Carmarthen, The Red Book of Hergest, The Book of Taliessin, and The Book of Aneirin (or Aneurin), all of which are, on the whole, of later date than the Irish. The Black Book was probably put together in the middle of the twelfth century. The Red Book is dated to the turn of the fourteenth and fifteenth centuries.

Both Taliessin arid Aneirin were supposedly sixth-century poets. The former wrote odes or *awdlau* eulogising the martial prowess of King Urien of Rheged, a minor kingdom in what is now Cumbria, his longest work being the *Cad Goddeu* or 'Battle of the Trees' which is held by some to retain Druidic elements. As nothing he composed was given written form until some 700 years after his death, it is impossible to know how much has been changed or lost. Aneirin's principal work was *Y Gododdin*, written in commemoration of a vain attempt to recapture the town of Catraeth (now Catterick in Yorkshire) from the Saxons.

Reference has already been made to those triplets called 'The Triads' and these should be explained. The oldest – though far from complete – collection goes back only to the thirteenth-century manuscript Peniarth 16, while the remainder are fragments in the *Black Book of Carmarthen,* the *White Book of Rhydderch,* and the *Red Book of Hergest.* However, despite late dating, they contain, as Rachel Bromwich says, matter of considerable antiquity. Indeed, their actual form suggests they were pre-literate, as triplets of this kind would have been a convenient mnemonic for those who had to memorise them and corresponds with similar mnemonic devices used to assist in remembering laws.

Unfortunately, the fullest collection, the *Triads of the Island of Britain* (Trioedd Ynys Prydein), first published in 1801 in the *Myvyrian Archaiology of Wales* and translated by W. Probert about 1823, is extremely dubious. It was assembled towards the end of the previous century by a man calling himself 'Iolo Morganwg,' in fact, the bardic pseudonym of Edward Williams, a stonemason working in London, He claimed them as part of a store of traditional Druidic lore which the bards of his native Glamorganshire alone had preserved uncorrupted down the centuries. While there is reason to think that some may be genuinely ancient, they have suffered at the hands of Williams who interpolated spurious matter not all of which is readily identifiable, making the panning of ore from dross virtually impossible

There is, of course, reason to suppose that a much larger repository of British Matter existed in the past. One indicator is the presence on the Continent of motifs which are not to be found in the British, but which are manifestly of Celtic origin. As we have seen, it has always been assumed that the source of this was those Welsh refugees who settled in Brittany at the Saxon Conquest. The possibility of a later route of transmission is opened up by Geoffrey Ashe's *The Discovery of King Arthur,* which seeks to demonstrate that the Continental campaigns with which Arthur is credited in some medieval sources are historical and left a detritus of legend behind them.

There are two further pieces of evidence. The first is the gaps in many of the existing recensions which often totally disrupt narrative coherence. In some cases, the copyists – or perhaps those who recited the stories to them

– have sought to make these good by inventions of their own, frequently implausible and out of keeping with the general ethos of their material. In one episode in 'Manawydan Son of Llyr,' for example, Pryderi and his mother, Rhiannon, enter a castle which has appeared out of the mist and then, in a roll of thunder, vanishes with them as prisoners. Manawydan – the Irish god Mananann, here portrayed as a kind of North Welsh land-owner – sets out to rescue them and succeeds only after an extraordinary and unlikely incident which has no logical connection with the previous events of the story. It obviously conceals extremely archaic matter which the teller has garbled or else rejected because he either disapproves of its paganism or does not understand its significance. Alternatively, it may be that, the original ending having been lost, another was tagged on, if only to account for the fact that Pryderi and Rhiannon are able to reappear in subsequent tales.

The second piece of evidence is the discovery by folklorists like Rhys, of motifs in rural Wales that parallel those occurring in the Irish myth cycles, though missing from the actual British Matter. In the *Tain Bo Cuailnge,* Cu Chulainn, occupied in a single-handed struggle against the hosts of Con-naught, rejects the untimely advances of Morrigan – the Morgan le Fay of the medieval Arthurian legends. Angered, she comes against him in three forms. One is that of an eel that coils itself round his legs when he is in mortal combat in the middle of a ford and most needs to keep his balance. Nowhere in the British stories does an eel occur, but Rhys mentions it in connection with the curative wells in Wales. A large eel was once said to have lived in the well at Llangybi where it coiled itself round the limbs of those undergoing treatment, supposedly thereby ensuring the efficacy of the cure.

In both cases – the first explicit and the second implicit – the eel is given a supernatural character like the salmon encountered earlier. In both cases it produces its effect by coiling round the legs of someone in water. Admittedly in the second it is beneficent where it is maleficent in the first, but this is only because of Cu Chulainn's ungallant conduct which, since the Morrigan is a war-goddess, was perhaps a little rash.

The story of Pryderi and Rhiannon, mentioned in the previous section, comes from the *Mabinogion,* a primary source which will be much cited hereafter. The *Mabinogion* or *Four Branches* is a collection of stories in prose which though they can accurately be called British are mostly set in Wales, a fact which in itself indicates that the existing versions are likely to date from after the Saxon invasion when the Britons had been squeezed into the western half of the country.

Some commentators have drawn attention to internal evidence imply-ing that originally the stories were located elsewhere and Rodney Castleden pursues S. F. Annett's hypothesis that 'Peredur, Son of Evrawg' might even have been set in the area of Sussex round Windover Hill, near where the famous hill-figure, the Wilmington Giant, is to be seen.

The name *Mabinogion* is the plural of *Mabinogi,* a word broadly translatable as 'childhood,' but with connotations that make it closer to the French *enfance.* It used to be held that these were stories which an apprentice-bard had to learn as part of his training. It is now accepted that it means a story describing the conception, birth, and early life of a particular hero.

The work's title is actually one of convenience rather than accuracy and was adopted soon after the first English translation, by lady Charlotte Guest in 1849. *Mabinogion,* within the definition just iterated, are the four first stories in most collections, which are in fact the Four Branches: 'Pwyll Lord of Dyfed,' 'Branwen Daughter of Llyr,' 'Manwydan Son or Llyr,' and 'Math Son of Mathonwy.' However, a further seven are usually now included. These are: 'The Dream of Maxen,' 'Lludd and Llevelys,' 'How Kulhwch won Olwen,' 'The Dream of Rhonabwy,' 'Owein,' 'Peredur Son of Evrawg,' and 'Gereint and Enid.'

Although at least two early manuscripts, the thirteenth-century Peniarth 6 and the fourteenth-century *White Book of Rhydderch,* exist, they are in varying states of dilapidation. Parts i and ii of Peniarth 6 has snatches of 'Branwen' and 'Manawydan,' and the *White Book,* which probably once contained all eleven stories, has only part of 'Lludd,' 'Kulhwch,' and 'Owein' in it, while 'Rhonabwy' is absent. This means that the earliest complete extant version is that of the *Red Book of Hergest,* which also contains a Welsh translation of Geoffrey of Monmouth's *History of the Kings of Britain.*

Whether the *Red Book* is a copy of the *White* or vice versa, or whether both derive from a common (lost) original, is disputed by scholars and the principal differences between the two manuscripts are minor, though there are some of order. In the Red Book it is 'Rhonabwy,' other matter, then 'Owein,' 'Peredur,' 'Maxen,' 'Lludd' followed by the Four Branches, 'Gereint' and 'Kulhwch.' In the White Book the Four Branches come first, followed by other material, then 'Peredur,' 'Maxen,' 'Lludd,' (probably) 'Rhonabwy,' 'Owein,' other material, then 'Gereint' and 'Kulhwch.'

Despite late dating, it would be a mistake to suppose the material is itself late, though some of it bears the marks of having been influenced by French courtly romance and uses French words. At least one, 'Kulhwch and Olwen,' has been tentatively dated to the eighth century.

The truth of Matthew Arnold's observation quoted earlier is most forcefully brought home when one looks through these medieval retellings. Here, indeed, the storyteller is like the Halicarnassian or *Ephesian* peasant building his hut from stones whose history is known merely by 'glimmering tradition.' In a sense, too, he is like those Italian and Flemish painters who represented events from the Gospels as though they had happened in their own cities and times. Yet, strangely enough, despite this, the Matter of Britain conserves early archaic, as we may say Druidic elements, not to be found in the Irish.

As for the remaining Celtic regions of the British Isles, Cornish ceased to be spoken as a language in the eighteenth century; Manx was lost somewhat later, and though there are still some speakers the only literature appears to have been oral, some having been anthologised usually in the form of stories for children.

Despite the disappearance of Cornish, there is at least one story – or more properly a cycle of stories – that can possibly be ascribed to the Duchy – those of Tristan and Isolt. The name 'Tristan' suggests some French influence, since it contains the French word *triste* (sad), given him because of his mother's death at his birth. However, in the view of Loomis it derives from the story of a Pictish king, Drust, which later reached Wales via Ireland, where most of its incidents are paralleled in the 'Grainme and Diarmait' story.

It certainly gives evidence of having passed through many hands before reaching the twelfth-century version, generally agreed to be the oldest in our possession and which is ascribed to Beroul.

The French scholar Joseph Bedier demonstrated in the last century that there had at one time been five primary versions of 'Tristan and Isolt' in circulation. Each preserved the main events in the same order, suggesting that they had originally been taken from a single prototype. At the same time, each differed from the other sufficiently to show they had all passed through a number of intermediary versions before reaching the pens of the authors of the five primary ones.

The controversy surrounding other aspects of the work extends to the identity of Beroul, and while there are innumerable theories on the subject no one has identified or located him with total conviction.

The reason for ascribing its origins to the Cornish peninsula rather than Wales is that it is here that most of the incidents are set. The moving of settings for reasons of local patriotism is by no means unknown, but the fact that German and French writers are at one lends support to the view Cornwall was probably the original location.

It has been necessary to dwell at some length on the origins of those transcriptions of the stories in our possession, and particularly the extreme lateness of their dating, as a warning against the temptation to draw unsupportable conclusions from them.

It must also be remembered that they are translations. The problem that any translator faces is that languages rarely offer an exact, one-to-one equivalence of vocabulary. There is no English equivalent for the French *sympathique,* for example, and no exact French equivalent for our word mind. The Celtic tongues are not modern, but ancient and obscure ones, containing words enshrining concepts that can often only be surmised at. The Celtic word 'geis' is usually translated as 'taboo,' but actually carried connotations not borne by our own word, itself imported from Polynesia.

A *geis* is also a 'fate' laid by one person, or sometimes a god, on another. If the myths are any guide, however unlikely its terms may be, a *geis* is destined to be broken, where the breaking of a taboo can be – and is – successfully avoided.

Taken all in all, one could say that the fact that we still possess so much of a literature originally conveyed wholly by word of mouth, often made accessible to us in excellent translations, is a kind of minor miracle. There is even hope that our hoard may be increased. At the beginning of the century a complete version of the 'Wooing of Etain' turned up in a copy of *The Yellow Book of Lecan* in – of all places! – Cheltenham.

Chapter 5

THE MATTER OF IRELAND

It is, naturally, impossible to offer more than a bald summary of a selection of the principal myths here and they should be read in the fuller versions in one of the many excellent translations now available.

Most Celtic myths comprise two intermeshing elements. There is the broad, overall narrative, whose point of departure is a particular event, as in the *Tain Bo Cuailnge* where it is Queen Mebd of Connaught's desire for the Ulstermen's Brown Bull. The preceding events and the ancestry of the Brown Bull, who is, in fact, the reincarnation of a magician-swineherd, are described while the war that follows serves as the excuse for telling other stories, some of which – such as 'The Intoxication of the Ulstermen' – seem at first sight to have little to do with the main narrative. This is concerned with the adventures of the hero Cu Chulainn, whose history from conception to the time he is thrown, single-handed, into the struggle to hold back the Connaught hosts, is also told in full, each of his battles against the enemy champions itself forming a separate story.

Even with the British Matter, where the overall narrative tends to be shorter, one often finds the same kind of treatment of separate adventures within a basic framework. The form is reminiscent of the serial and probably indicates that the tellers spread their material over a succession of episodes told on separate evenings, perhaps as a means of increasing income.

The Irish tradition comprises four myth cycles.

The first is devoted to the five prehistoric invasions of Ireland, all but the last by divinities. The earliest settlers were the Race of Partholon, named after their king. Accompanied by his queen Dealgnaid, twenty-four males, and an equal number of females, Partholon landed, significantly enough, on 1 May, the Festival of Beltaine. They had come from some western land, exiled by invaders or natural disaster. Insofar as they may actually have existed it has been suggested that they were possibly the Neolithic megalith builders.

For the Celts, the west was the direction from which came all wonders, but the storytellers identify it with Spain. Robert Graves, among others, has suggested that if they came from the Iberian peninsula at all it was by way of Greece. His evidence is the similarity between many of the Irish Neolithic tombs with those found in Crete and Mycenae, the use in the decoration of both of the labyrinth pattern and the name 'Partholon,' whose initial P, frequent in Greek, would have been rare in Irish Celtic where it would have been mutated into a Q or hard C. It is certainly true that, from the trail left by their monuments, the megalith builders did indeed follow the west coast of Europe.

The Partholonians' story tells how, as they grew in number, so the area of Ireland, at first a single grassless plain broken by three lakes and nine rivers, grew not only in size, but in beauty and fertility. They waged successful war against a series of aggressors, particularly the malevolent Fomors, a tribe of giants, and lived in Ireland for 5,000 years, finally to be wiped out within the space of a week by a plague. Only one man, Tuan mac Cairill, survived and so was able to preserve their history, with that of subsequent invasions, centuries later.

According to his version, the demise of the Partholonians having left Ireland untenanted, it was next colonised by the Race of Nemed, who continued the work of enlargement between further struggles with the Fomors, who in many ways parallel the Titans of Greek mythology. A fresh outbreak of plague then afflicted the Race of Nemed and, though without the annihilating results of that which had destroyed their predecessors, left them so weakened they had to accept Fomorian dominance and the heavy exactions they laid upon them.

Most intolerable of these was the yielding up for sacrifice of two thirds of their children. In the end, they were provoked to revolt. At first victorious, the numerical superiority of the Fomors proved too great and, in the struggle, they were reduced from 16,000 to a mere thirty, though some accounts say they perished entirely. However, even thirty was insufficient to maintain the most tenuous hold on Ireland, which they then vacated.

The next settlers were the four tribes of Fir Bolgs, whom some authorities have equated with the Belgae – that is to say, the ancestors of today's Belgians. It was they who first divided Ireland into four provinces, giving one to each tribe. Although the Fir Bolgs seem to have joined forces with the Fomorians, and thus to be yet another race of mythical rather than actual colonisers, as late as the seventeenth century there were said to be those, particularly in Connaught, who claimed Fir Bolg descent. This is taken as support for the theory of their actuality, but the tracing of tribal ancestries back to divine races is universal and was certainly practised among the Celts, for it was exciting scepticism in the times of Gerald of Wales (the late twelfth century) and continued among Scottish Highland clan-lairds well into the nineteenth.

The confinement of the Fir Bolgs within a single province was due to the next arrivals, the Tuatha De Danann. Freely translated, this means the People of the Goddess Dana,' but the name is variously rendered as Danu, Ana, Anu and, in the Welsh myths, as Don.

Jeffrey Gantz suggests that the invasion stories may be associated with the succession of the pastoral-hunters by the agriculturists or of Neolithic peoples by those of the Bronze Age. However, the evidence is thin and, to some extent, ambiguous, though there is some to link the Tuatha with iron-working, which was said to be one of the many civilising gifts they brought with them. Others included medicine, magic, and poetry. It was presumably as a result of the ability to smelt iron that the Celts were able to fabricate the plough, which was instrumental in increasing their agricultural productivity.

They also brought four chief treasures. The sword of Nuada, fatal at every stroke; the fiery, blood dripping spear of Lugh; the inexhaustible cauldron of Dagda; and the Stone of Destiny, which has been tentatively identified as the one forming part of the coronation chair on which British monarchs are crowned. Jessie Weston links the four Tuathan gifts with the suits of the Tarot, but while swords are among these, and the cauldron may correspond with the suit of cups and the spear of Lugh possibly with that of wands, it is not easy to see how the Stone of Destiny could have become the fourth suit, that of pentacles, On the whole, one can go no further than other writers who have seen the Tuatha, with their gifts and treasures, as representing the Celtic reverence for science, technology, poetry, and artistic skill given practical form through the class of *aes dana,* which, of course, incorporates the name of the founding goddess of the Tuatha.

But like the Partholonians and Nemedians, the Tuatha soon found themselves engaged in war with the Fomorians. The First Battle of Mag Tuireadh, though conducted according to the strict etiquette governing all Celtic wars, ended in terrible slaughter. In the end the superior magic of the Tuatha and their 'beautifully-shaped, slender, long, sharp-pointed spears' overcame the heavier, thicker ones of the Fir Bolg, a detail taken as further corroboration that the Tuatha were iron-users whose weapons were pitted against more cumbersome and inefficient flint ones. To some, among them Squires, it suggests that the First Battle of Mag Tuireadh was historical.

At the end of a long and savage engagement, the Fomorian dead were said to be more numerous than 'the snow-flakes of winter or the waves of the tempest,' their graves marked by the standing-stones at Carrowmore, Co. Sligo. However, the Tuatha had their casualties, too, among them their king, Nuada, who lost a hand. Though replaced by a silver prosthesis made by the divine physician Diancecht, because of the requirement that a king should be without physical defect, he was forced to abdicate, like Bress as the result of Coirpre's *glam.*

And in fact it was precisely this turn of fortune which brought Bress, son of the Fomorian king, to the throne offered him by the Tuatha in a gesture of reconciliation towards their erstwhile enemies. As Bress proved to be tyrant as well as miser, they soon had cause to repine their magnanimity and a means of deposing him was sought. A combination of events brought this about. As we saw, Coirpre's *glam* brought him out in blotches, while at the same time Cian, Diancecht's son and an even more skilled physician than his father, managed to restore Nuada's severed hand. Thus he was able to reclaim the throne, while a reluctant and aggrieved Bress departed to his father's undersea kingdom to gather an avenging army.

Once more the Tuatha made their war plans, dividing the various tasks among themselves according to ability. It was at this moment that a handsome young god appeared at Nuada's door. He was Lugh, surnamed the Many-Skilled because of his wide-ranging talents which included carpentery, forging in iron and bronze, fighting, playing the harp, story-telling, medicine and sorcery, as well as playing the board-game *Fidchell* in which he invented a new gambit known as 'Lugh's enclosure.'

Fidchell, *gwyddbwyll* in the British Matter, recurs in the mythology and, as in Squires, is often interpreted as 'chess.' However, Tolstoy is undoubtedly correct in maintaining that the mythical games such as the one just cited and in 'The Dream of Rhonabwy' and 'Peredur' are ritualistic. In 'The Dream of Rhonabwy' the fortunes on the boards seem to be paralleled by those on an off-stage battlefield. Examples of games between Other World players producing correspondences in the mortal realm are to be found in mythologies world-wide and Idris Llewelyn Foster, in an article in Arthurian *Literature in the Middle Ages,* compares *gwyddbwyll* with the 'game of the gods' in the Scandinavian *Voluspa*, where, as here and elsewhere in Celtic mythology, the pieces are gold. It is through such games that the gods maintain order in the world.

While preparations for the new war were afoot Cian, son of the physician Dianchecht, described as the father of Lugh, was caught while in the open by his enemies, the three sons of Tuirenn. Knowing they would try to kill him, he sought to evade them by changing himself into a pig, but magic hounds flushed him out and he was slain. The murdered body having been found by Lugh, he called an assembly of the Tuathans, at which the sons of Tuirenn were present, to decide what compensation was due.

Most of the gods favoured capital punishment for the culprits once they had been unmasked, but Lugh said he would accept a blood-fine instead and the sons of Tuirenn, fearful he might change his mind, and support demands for their deaths, confessed.

They were then set a list of tasks. They were to procure three apples, a pig-skin, a spear, a two-horse chariot, seven pigs, a hound-whelp, a cooking-spit and three shouts on a hill.

At first amazed by this leniency they were less so as Lugh began to enunciate the nature of each item. The three apples were the magic ones from the Garden of Hesperides which did not diminish as they were eaten. The pig-skin was that of Tuis, king of Greece, which restored the wounded and when used as a strainer turned water into wine. The spear belonged to Pisear, king of Persia, and must be kept in a barrel of water or it would burn down the town in which it was stored. The chariot was owned by Dobhar, King of Sicily, and could run on land or sea. The seven pigs were those of Easal, King of the Golden Pillars, which though killed every night were alive on the morrow; the hound-whelp that of the King of Ioruaidhe who caught every beast she chased; the cooking-spits those of the women of Fianchuive. Finally the place where they were to give their three shouts was Miodhchaoin's Hill, though Miodhchaoin and his three sons, the same fierce warriors who trained Lugh himself in arms, would slay any who so trespassed.

The sons of Tuirenn now realised the extreme difficulty of acquiring these items and the reluctance of their owners to part with them. They succeeded by employing to the utmost their own magical gifts – for example, by changing themselves into hawks to swoop on the orchard and steal the apples in the Garden of Hesperides. In Greece and Persia they passed themselves off as bards and demanded first the pig-skin and then King Pisear's spear in payment. In Sicily they enlisted as mercenaries in the army of King Dobhar and, by means of a ruse, when shown the magic chariot overcame its driver and made their own getaway in it. The other tasks were completed either by these means or by mortal combat.

At last they had only the three shouts left and went to Miodhchaoin's Hill to carry out this last task. Miodhchaoin himself was lying in wait, but was killed, whereupon his own sons came to avenge him and drive their spears into the bodies of the three sons of Tuirenn, who simultaneously drove theirs into the bodies of Miodhchaoin's sons, killing them.

Though grievously wounded, the sons of Tuirenn were able to reach home and beg their father to intervene with Lugh in their behalf. The sun god was unrelenting and the three of them died, leaving their father to mourn their passing.

Lists of apparently impossible tasks are not infrequent in most mythologies. In the Greek there are the famous 'Twelve Labours of Hercules,' suggesting that all such stories may stem from a common, primitive origin. However, although another is to be found in the very early 'Kulhwch and Olwen,' discussed in the next chapter, and, in modified form, in 'The Courtship of Cu Chulainn,' Dillon believes the story to be late. The classical allusions, such as to 'Tuis, King of Greece,' which could just conceivably be a debased form of 'Theseus, King of Athens,' seem to support this. In any event, nowhere in Greek mythology is it implied that the apples of the Hesperides, the procuring of which is one of the Labours of Hercules, possess the characteristic of not diminishing when eaten. On the other hand, there is at least one Celtic apple which does: the one given to Connla son of Conn by an Other World woman. As pig-skins and spears are also markedly Celtic, it is likely that the story was given its Greek and Persian touches by a storyteller anxious to impart a cachet of scholarship to his work.

During the seven years of war planning, the Fomorians had continued to exact tribute from the Tuathans. Matters were brought to a head when Lugh slaughtered the Fomorian tax-gatherers, sparing only nine out of the twenty-seven that they might return with news of how they had been treated. The Fomorians could not refuse such a challenge and there followed the Second Battle of Mag Tuireadh in which, after another long and bloody struggle, the Fomorians were routed.

Unlike the first battle, there is nothing to indicate this conflict's historicity. Squires goes so far as to suggest it was a medieval invention, perhaps that of a writer who had heard legends of some ancient battle on the site As he points out, the earliest documents refer only to a single battle.

The Tuatha did not long enjoy the fruits of victory, for soon fresh invaders were arriving, not this time divine, but mortal, the ancestors of the Gaels themselves, led by their king, Mile.

The Milesians advanced on Tara, the Tuathan capital which stood at the epicentre of Ireland. Again a battle following the Celtic rules of fair play ensued and, after a struggle of competing magics, the newcomers were victorious.

Some of the defeated gods left Ireland for the west. Others, including the Dagda, king of the gods, moved into the sidhs, the prehistoric burial mounds, while a few, such as Manannan (the British Manawydan), divided their time between their new western homeland, Ireland and other places, one of which was the Isle of Man, to which he gave his name. However, as the conquerors failed to make a peace treaty, the remaining Tuathans continued to harass them with their magic, curdling the milk in the buckets and blighting crops. Only when the Milesians undertook to pay the homage due to divinities did the Tuatha cease these annoyances.

From this time on relations between men and gods continued on a reasonably amicable basis. There were even marriages between them. An instance is that of Macha in the *Tain Bo Cuailnge* who one day turns up at the home of the widower Crunniac mac Agnomain of Ulster. Ravishingly beautiful, she was welcomed into his home where, besides fulfilling all the duties of a wife, including that of lover, she magically provides food and clothing for Crunniac and his children.

There is one condition: though she can run like the wind her husband was under geis never to ask her to demonstrate her skill. While at the races he rashly boasts that his wife can outrun any horse there and accepts an imprudent wager to prove it. To save his honour Macha is forced to compete despite her pregnancy. She wins, but collapses on the track and there and then bears twins, the Emain Macha, thus giving a name to the place where it happened and, somewhat incongruously, to a hymn-tune. The pangs of labour which befall the men of Ulster in their time of greatest need are her punishment.

Such stories of liaisons between mortals and Other World begins, in later times usually called fairies, terminated by the inevitable breaking of a *geis,* as Rhys shows, had their counterpart in Welsh folk-legend.

Other stories come down to us from this period of what might be called 'the exile of the gods.' Typical is 'The Dream of Oengus.' Oengus (or Angus) mac Oc becomes enamoured of the beautiful woman who haunts his dreams but who dissolves the moment he tries to seize her in his arms. Wasting away from unrequited love, his parents seek the aid of the Dagda, who institutes a search. For a year it is unsuccessful, then Oengus is summoned to an assembly of young women and among the 'thrice fifty' – a customary Celtic rendering of numbers – he picks out his dream-woman Caer, daughter of Etal Ambuel.

But Caer cannot give him her love, for she is a swan-maiden who at summer's end, the Celtic feast of Samain, will resume avian form. The persistent Oengus waits until she has taken on her swan-shape and goes down to the shores of the lake where he sees her with her friends, all now swans, gliding over the dark surface of the water. There he proclaims his passion and is accepted, providing he too will become a swan. He agrees; as Caer approaches, he is transformed into a handsome cob and the couple take wing. Three times they circle the lake before making for Oengus's palace, and as they wheel they sing the Noble Strain which lulls all onlookers to sleep.

The second great Gaelic cycle is that of the Ulster heroes and their champion Cu Chulainn. Besides his mortal father Sualdam, he is also said to be the son of Lugh made pregnant by his mother Dechtine, daughter and charioteer to King Conchobhar, after she drinks the magical fluid he gives her. Such cases of dual-paternity are, of course, common in mythology. Aethra, mother of Theseus, becomes pregnant when she sleeps with King Aegeus of Athens, but that same night she goes to the temple of Poseidon at Poros, where she is seduced by the god, so that her son is able to claim both mortal and divine parentage.

Like Hercules, preternaturally strong from birth, Cu Chulainn gained his nickname, meaning 'Hound of Chulainn,' when, at the age of six, he killed the gigantic watchdog of the smith Chulainn which had attacked him. Thereafter he undertakes to guard Chulainn's house until another has been trained. As a consequence of this he was placed under a *geis* never to eat the flesh of dog.

His hearing was so acute that, overhearing the great Druid Cathbad some miles away telling students that the boy who took up arms that day would have a short but heroic life, he went to his patron, King Conchobhar, and, though still only seven, demanded first to be armed then given a chariot. He not only takes over the protection of the province from his foster-father, Conall Cernach, but with the king's charioteer, Ibor, embarks on a mad spree in which he kills numerous enemies.

When he is spotted on his way back to the king's court he is in the throes of the first of his famous and terrifying battle-furies. In this, one of his eyes sinks back into his head while the other becomes as big as a saucer, his joints reverse themselves, his hair sticks up in spikes like nails, bringing to mind the Celtic warriors' custom of stiffening their hair with lime. He generates so much heat that the snow melts for a yard round where he sits or, if he is put into a bath of cold water, he causes it to boil.[4]

Hoping to calm him, Conchobhar orders the women to strip and go forward to meet him. This has been taken as indicative of sexual precocity, but in fact the use of naked women to calm angry warriors is found in other cultures.

In due course he falls in love with the beautiful Emer, who agrees to marry him if he can wrest her from her possessive father, Forgall, and her kindred. Hearing of the betrothal, Forgall plans to get rid of his daughter's suitor by having him sent to the Amazon Scathach for martial training, believing the difficulties of the journey to be such that he would perish en route. However, Cu Chulainn endures its perils and even masters the bridge leading to Scathach's lair which stands on end the moment foot is set on it.

Returning as a trained warrior he storms Forgall's palace, killing all who try to obstruct him, and seizes Emer.

But his greatest challenge comes when Queen Mebd of Connaught tries to acquire the magic Brown Bull of Ulster. Refused it by its owner, she resorts to force and begins assembling her armies.

It is then, just as Macha had threatened, that the Ulstermen are overtaken by her curse and fall into debilitating lassitude. Only Cu Chulainn is young enough to escape and for days keeps the hosts at bay single-handed, hoping to delay them until the Ulstermen recover. When time passes and there is no sign of this happening, he proposes to meet the Connaught champions one at a time in single combat. Mebd agrees because her losses have been such that, as she succinctly puts it, 'It is better to lose one man a day than a hundred.'

Again and again, Mebd sends her best men against him and again and again Cu Chulainn despatches them, including, most reluctantly, his old friend, the Connaught champion Fergus, and his fellow student under Scathach, Ferdia. Not even Mebd and Ailill's offer of the hand of their daughter Finnabair to Cu Chulainn's killer can produce anyone capable of the deed.

---

4 A comparison has frequently been made between this and the Germanic *Wut* which, in many ways, it resembles.

However, even Cu Chulainn is unsuccessful in stopping a raid by a detachment of Mebd's army, which captures the Brown Bull.

At last, his whole body covered in wounds and weakened from loss of blood, his divine father Lugh takes him from the battle to tend him. He is replaced by a band of cadets, who, though they wreak terrible havoc on the invaders, are in the end themselves annihilated. Cu Chulainn, now recovered, immediately avenges them.

Her champions having failed her, Mebd next turns to magic, sending the fierce and terrible Calatin to bewitch and kill Cu Chulainn. The fight is so desperately unequal that some of the Connaught host throw themselves in on Cu Chulainn's side and kill the magicians. But it is then that the Morrigan, knowing of his exploits, offers her aid in return for his love. Spurned, she comes against him as an eel to trip him, a she-wolf to rend him, and a hornless red heifer to trample him. Although engaged in a life-and-death struggle with yet another Connaught champion, Loch, Cu Chulainn overcomes the Morrigan's malevolence and defeats his opponent into the bargain.

After further single combats, the Ulster hero is again in extremis and there is no sign of his compatriots recovering from the Macha's curse. Desperate, his mortal father, Sualdam, tries to rouse his compatriots. He fails until beheading himself accidentally, his disembodied head goes on calling them to arms. The macabre sight of his blood-streaming head finally shakes them from their lethargy. The hosts are summoned and the invaders driven off amid great slaughter.

Mebd tries, unsuccessfuly, to keep the Brown Bull, but peace is made between the warring provinces on condition it is returned.

There follow a succession of episodes in the life of Cu Chulainn, some heroic, some describing his amorous adventures like that with the sidh-goddess Fand, wife of Mananann, to whose land he travels. She, though besotted with passion, abandons him after a moving appeal from Emer.

But Mebd's hatred of the Ulster champion is implacable and again she begins to encompass his destruction by magic. First, she drives him into madness so that he believes himself under attack by phantom armies. When, through the counter-magic of Cathbad, he recovers, other means are tried: while away from home, he is told that Ulster has come under attack once more, its towns ravaged and plundered, its children killed, its women raped.

Despite the appeals of his charioteer, Loeg, he takes up the three spears of which it was prophesied each would kill a king, and insists on being driven to where the enemy is to be found.

The auguries of death are fast gathering round his head. A woman he sees washing blood-soaked clothes at a ford tells him they belong to Cu Chulainn. Then he comes on three hags hunched round a cooking pot.

They beg him to stay and eat with them and, when he refuses, reproach him for feasting with the rich, while disdaining the hospitality of the poor. Shamed, he joins them. But the meat in their pot is dog, the flesh forbidden by his *geis*. He rises from the meal with half his body paralysed.

As he does, he sees chariots approaching. First, three Druids come to him and ask for his spears, threatening to satirise him in a *glam* if he refuses.

He fulfils their request by thrusting a spear into the body of each one of them.

Enemies are now all round. One retrieves the last of the spears and with it inflicts a fatal wound. His charioteer, who has tried to fight for him, has already been killed. His mare flings herself on the attackers, killing eight of them before she is herself killed.

Cu Chulainn has meanwhile bound himself to a standing stone by means of his belt that he might die on his feet. As the mare perishes, so too the hero light dies from Cu Chulainn's eyes. According to tradition he was twenty-seven years old.

The storytellers divided their matter into various categories. Besides destructions, invasions, battles, cattle raids and elopements there were the voyages. Into this category fall such tales as 'The Voyages of Maeldun' with its accounts of visits to mythical wonderlands and magical islands, such as the Island of Pigs, the Island of Apples, or the Island of the Glass Bridge.

Magic islands are notably Celtic and show an extraordinary persistence. Gerald of Wales describes with a perfectly straight face Irish islands on which no one dies, where no female animal may enter, ones that are haunted by good or evil spirits and one where corpses left in the open do not putrefy. In Wales, too, there was a widely-held belief in magic islands whose inhabitants had the power to whisk certain individuals off to their domains with the speed of thought.

There is one further myth cycle of pagan times: that of the hero Finn of mac Cumhail.

Finn is leader of a warrior band called the Fianna. Whereas the Cu Chulainn stories are set mostly in Ulster, the location of this cycle is two of the other provinces, Leinster and Munster, though Connaught continues, as in *Tain Bo Cuailnge*, to be the main enemy. Like the Ulster champion, Finn is a hero even in boyhood. The stories are series of adventures mostly heroic, but some amorous, such as that of 'Grainme and Diarmait.'

Finn, wishing for a wife, visits the court of the High King of Ireland to sue for the hand of his daughter, Grainme. But at a banquet, Grainme glimpses and falls hopelessly in love with Diarmait, a member of Finn's party. Having drugged the other guests, she confesses her passion to Diarmait. He rejects her on the grounds she is promised to Finn, but she lays a *geis* on him whereby he must elope with her.

That night the couple slip away, soon to be pursued by a furious Finn. Twice he and his band catch up with and surround the fugitives and twice they escape through the intervention of friendly gods. In the end a reconciliation is arranged and Diarmait and Grainme return to the embrace of their Fenian comrades who have been sympathetically disposed towards them all along.

But secretly Finn is unrelenting. He incites Diarmait to hunt a dangerous wild boar. He kills it, but Finn, who knows that, like Achilles, he is vulnerable through his heel, persuades Diarmait to pace out the size of the skin with bare feet. A bristle pierces the flesh, inflicting a poisoned wound from which Diarmait dies.

The stories continue with those of Finn's son Oisin, who has the same mysterious genesis as other heroes. His mother Sadb is transformed into a deer, accounting for his name which means 'Pawn.' However, found by Finn's dog, he is immediately recognised by Finn as his son.

Although Oisin has been referred to as 'the poet of the Fianna,' and as such provided the inspiration, if not the actual matter, for Scottish James Macpherson's eighteenth-century 'Ossianic Ballads,' which include 'Fingal' and 'Temora,' there is no sanction in the myths for belief in his poetic skill.

Oisin is the father of Oscar, killed at the Battle of Gabra, when the Fianna themselves are overcome and destroyed. Oisin took no part in the battle, for the lovely Niamh, having fallen in love with him, comes out of the western sea on her white steed to entice him to accompany her to Tir na n'Og. Though grieved at leaving his now ageing father, he was unable to bring himself to refuse and lived for perhaps a hundred, perhaps a thousand years in this joyful land.

But the desire to see old companions is, in the end, irresistible. Despite the pleadings of Niamh, who knew the fate awaiting mortals rash enough to return to their own world, he persuades her to lend him her remarkable white horse, though she warns him not to descend from the saddle.

On it he returns to Ireland, only to find himself surrounded by desolation. Those he knew are long since dead; palaces and castles stand in ruins. Worse, he does what he has been specifically cautioned against doing – he dismounts. Some versions say that this was because he came upon a great stone trough he recognised as that of the Fianna and got down to examine it more closely. Others say that he attempted to help some men who were trying to raise a huge stone. In either event, the minute he touched earth, he was a withered old man, half blind and spent, while Niamh's horse galloped back to Tir na n'Og. The Oisinic cycle takes the myths down to Christian times and in some traditions Oisin is supposed to have met and been converted by St. Patrick.

Chapter 6

THE MATTER OF BRITAIN

Stylistically the stories in the British Matter are very different from the Irish, which are largely cyclic in character with individual adventures embedded in the mould of a broader narrative. In the *Tain Bo Cuailnge*, for example, each of Cu Chulainn's single combats represents a separate story and no doubt formed an evening's entertainment, but the whole is given unity by the underlying plot of Queen Mebd's attempt to acquire the Brown Bull.

The British stories are episodic, comparatively short, and in many what unifying thread there is is tenuous. Most have as their title the name of the principal character, as for example 'Manawydan Son of Llyr' or 'Math Son of Mathonwy', and they usually contain several events involving him. However, in some cases, such as 'Math', after one or two episodes, this character may be pushed into a subsidiary position or even abandoned altogether as the storyteller turns his attention to others.

As already pointed out, the climate of opinion in which the British material was transcribed was totally different from the one obtaining in Ireland, affecting attitudes towards the past and hence the way the stories were edited. All the same, pagan elements survive. Thus, in the first episode of 'Pwyll Lord of Dyfed' the eponymous hero while out hunting, meets Arawn, Lord of Annwvyn, the underworld, who complains of the persecution he is suffering at the hands of Havgan and promises Pwyll friendship in return for assistance in overcoming him. They then and there seal a bargain. For a year Pwyll will not only take over Arawn's realm, but also his physical appearance. At the end he is to meet and defeat Havgan in single combat, which as in the Cu Chulainn stories will take place at a ford, the usual arena for such encounters.

Why Arawn cannot fight his own battles and why it is necessary for Pwyll to take on his appearance is never made clear, but all goes according to plan. Magically transformed into the likeness of Arawn, Pwyll rules Annwvyn, living in its splendid palace with its beautiful queen, who is among those deceived by the exchange, but whom he nobly refuses to touch. She, believing it is her husband who is shunning her, is mortified and angry.

At the appointed time Pwyll meets and overcomes Havgan, though sparing his life. He and Arawn meet again and revert to their proper shapes. Returning to his offended wife, Arawn explains the deception and the reason for it. She, in her turn, tells him how Pwyll had refused to take advantage of her and both are deeply impressed by this display of integrity. Pwyll, on his own return to Dyfed, begins making discreet inquiries about its governance during an absence only he knew had taken place and is told that it had never been so justly and benevolently ruled.

This is only the first of Pwyll's encounters with mysterious beings. One day, while a feast is being held at his court, he decides to take a walk as far as a nearby tumulus, a place redolent with Other World influences, and corresponding, of course, with the Irish *sidhs*. As he is sitting on the mound he sees a woman on a pale horse riding slowly along the road below them. Pwyll sends one of his men in pursuit but, though the messenger goes as quickly as he can and the rider seems to move no faster, he is unable to catch up with her. In the end Pwyll has the fastest horse in his stables harnessed.

Still the strange rider cannot be overtaken and, frustrated, the party returns to the court. Twice more Pwyll visits the tumulus, each time he sees the woman and each time pursues her in vain. It is only when he begs her to stop in the name of whom she loves best that she does so, allows Pwyll to approach, and identifies herself as Rhiannon.

The slow rider who cannot be overtaken – there are instances in the Irish Matter – is invariably an Other World one, for, as in Tir na n'Og, time and hence speed is quite different from that known to mortals.

Pwyll is overwhelmed by Rhiannon's beauty but she tells him she has been promised against her will to another, Gwawl. When Pwyll makes clear his eagerness to rescue and make her his own she proposes a plan which he undertakes to put into effect. Thereafter the story degenerates into knockabout farce. During a feast to mark her betrothal, a beggar turns up at Gwawl's hall begging for enough food to fill his bag. With surprising generosity, Gwawl agrees, and though more and more of the dishes prepared for the banquet disappear, the bag remains unfilled. Finally, the host is driven to protest and is told that only if a nobleman gets in the bag and presses down the contents will it be replete. Gwawl, deceived, gets in, whereupon the bag is pulled up over his head and tied. Pwyll casts off his rags, sounds his horn and his followers, who have surrounded the hall, rush in and overpower Gwawl's retainers.

The man in the bag becomes a football until he complains at the indignity of such a death and is released on giving sureties. Rhiannon is now Pwyll's and they 'repaired immediately to the bedchamber to pass the night in delight.'

From then on Pwyll, with Rhiannon as consort, rules Dyfed prosperously for two years, though the queen produces no heir until the third, when she bears a son. Soon after his birth, however, the queen's serving-woman carelessly falls asleep and the child vanishes. To avert guilt, the woman daubs the sleeping mother's face with animal blood and leaves bones littering the room, to give the impression she herself has destroyed it.

Believing this is indeed what has happened, the king decides to punish her by ordering her to sit for seven years by the mounting block at the entrance of his court to carry visitors to it on her back.

The scene now changes to the stable of Teirnon Twrvliant, lord of Gwent Ys Coed, owner of a magnificent mare which has foaled every May Eve, though no one has ever seen the offspring, which are always immediately stolen. This particular year, Teirnon has decided to conceal himself in the stable and there observe events. No sooner has the mare delivered than a huge hand reaches through the stable window to seize the newborn animal. With a blow of his sword, Teirnon hacks off the hand and rushes out to discover its owner.

The culprit has vanished, but Teirnon finds a babe swaddled in silk brocade which indicates it has come from a noble family. At first his childless wife tries to adopt it as their own, but when Teirnon hears of the disappearance of Pwyll's child he sees the resemblance between the boy and his father, concludes it must be his and returns it, thus liberating Rhiannon from her punishment.

The boy, already named Golden Hair by Teirnon and his wife, is now renamed Pryderi and, in due course, succeeds Pwyll as ruler of Dyfed.

A frequent motif of the British Matter is the hunt. It is, of course, while hunting that Pwyll encounters Arawn. The underworld nature of the latter is made clear by the colours of the hounds in his pack – luminous white with red ears. Brilliant whiteness is always associated with celestial creatures and red is the Celtic death colour.

The hunt setting recurs in 'Manawydan Son of Llyr.' Llyr is the British form of the Irish sea-god Ler, who provided Geoffrey of Monmouth with his 'King Leir' and Shakespeare with his 'Lear.' (His son, Manawydan, is the Irish Mananann, who appears in the Irish epics as the cuckolded husband of Fand with whom Cu Chulainn falls in love.)

In 'Manawydan Son of Llyr' we again meet Pryderi. As in 'Pwyll' and other stories, the hunting-field again provides the starting point for a series of mysterious events. Pryderi's hounds enter an unfamiliar copse, only to come whimpering and trembling to seek protection among the men. They find that the cause of the animals' distress is a shining white boar which leads the hunters on, racing ahead and then waiting for them to catch up. Finally, both quarry and dogs, who have now taken up the chase again, disappear through the gates of a strange grey castle, whereupon the baying hounds fall silent.

Leaving the rest of the field, Pryderi goes in and finds himself in a splendid, though deserted, marble court in the middle of which a fountain is playing and a golden bowl hangs from four chains extending upwards until lost to sight. Taken with the magnificence of the bowl, Pryderi makes straight for it, but as he touches it his hand sticks to it and his feet to the marble When he fails to reappear, his mother Rhiannon follows him inside and, seeing his predicament, tries to go to his aid, only to find herself stuck in the same way. The storyteller goes on: 'And when night fell, there came thunder and a great mist. And the castle vanished and, with it Pryderi and Rhiannon.'

After Pryderi and Rhiannon's disappearance, the action shifts to Manawydan, who, having failed to find the missing couple, takes upon himself the care of Pryderi's young wife

The story's highly unsatisfactory denouement has already been mentioned. While Manawydan is executing a mouse that has been stealing his corn, a bishop appears on the scene and, in exchange for the life of a creature which, he claims, is the bewitched form of his pregnant wife, agrees to remove the enchantment by which Pryderi and Rhiannon have disappeared, explaining that it was an act of revenge by Rhiannon's former betrothed, Gwawl, against her and against the son of the man who had humiliated him and stolen his bride-to-be. This is nonsense and gives the impression of having been cobbled together, partly to introduce a Christian element in the shape of the bishop, but mainly because the copyists did not understand the significance of the material.

The idea of the imprisonment of a young man recurs in 'Kulhwch and Olwen.' The story, which may date back to the eighth century, besides being the first to number a king named Arthur in its dramatis *personae,* also includes a huge cast, among whom are the recognizable names of gods, and even Irish heroes.

Kulhwch, the suitor of Olwen, goes with his companions, including Arthur, to her giant father Ysbaddaden. Ysbaddaden has many affinities with the Irish Balor, one of them being that his eyelids are so heavy that they have to be opened by servants. Like Lugh in 'The Sons of Tuirenn,' the giant sets Kulhwch a list of tasks. One is the freeing of Mabon ap Modron, literally 'Son, son of Mother,' but more often interpreted as 'The Young Son' and therefore analogous to the Irish Oengus Mac Oc (roughly 'Son of the Young' or 'The Young Son'), wooer of the swan-maiden, Caer. Mabon has been abducted from his mother when three nights old and has remained a prisoner, an echo not only of Pryderi's abduction in the previous tale but also of 'Pwyll,' since Rhiannon's infant was also mysteriously abducted on the third night of his life. Mabon, like Pryderi, is finally discovered in a strange castle, though, in the case of the former, only after the Druid Gwyrhyr has consulted various familiar creatures, including an eagle and salmon.

'Kulhwch and Olwen' is linked with 'Manawydan Son of Llyr' in another way, too: the hunt for a boar. In this case it is Twrc Trwyth and it is only after Modron's release that the hunt properly gets under way. After many desperate adventures and much slaughter, the creature is finally killed. The association of boar and underworld is strong and is also found in 'Math Son of Mathonwy', part of which seems to be an account of the introduction of pork into the British diet. News is brought to Math, Lord of Gwynedd, that these new and delicious animals are to be found at the court of Pryderi, who had received them as a gift from the underworld lord Arawn. Math covets them and to gratify him the magician Gwydion, whose possible identification with Odin has already been mentioned, tricks Pryderi into exchanging them for the horses and greyhounds he conjures into existence. With the pigs, Gwydion and his companions flee from Pryderi's court before they dissolve. When the deception is discovered the incensed Pryderi sets out in pursuit with his army, but the pig-rustlers find sanctuary in Gwynedd. A war follows in which Pryderi himself is killed in single combat with Gwydion.

The story continues with a number of unrelated incidents. Earlier Gwydion, in Math's absence, had raped Goewin, Math's footholder, a position which only a virgin could hold. Math punishes Gwydion and his accomplice in the crime, Gilvaethy, by turning them first into a hind and a stag who have to mate with one another, then into a boar and sow, finally into a wolf and she-wolf. The offspring of the couplings are taken into Math's court and baptised, while Gwydion and Gilvaethy are considered to have been sufficiently punished and are taken back into the court.

Having lost her maidenhood, Goewin must be replaced, and Arianrhod is proposed for the post. She so far fails the virginity test as actually to drop a baby boy, which Gwydion snatches up and hides.

Arianrhod refuses to name the child. Disguising the boy and himself and conjuring up a ship, Gwydion sails to Arianrhod's castle, Caer Arianrhod. Traditionally this is in North Wales and Rhys speaks of it as being known to locals of his time as Tregar Anthreg. But it was also the name given to the ellipse of northerly stars more familiarly known as the *Corona Borealis*.

Once there, Gwydion passes himself off as a cobbler and is engaged to make Arianrhod a pair of shoes. Going aboard for a fitting, she sees but does not recognise her son, who tosses a stone at a wren and hits it in the leg. Amazed at his aim, she exclaims: 'The light one has a skilled hand.' Thus is she tricked into giving him the name Lleu Law Gyffes, Lleu of the Skilful Hand. (Lleu = Light) has the same meaning as the Irish Lugh, who was given the same nickname, though in the Irish version the reason is quite different, which suggests that one or possibly both were late inventions. Angered by the deceit worked upon her, Arianrhod next swears not to arm him, but is forced to do so when Gwydion conjures up imaginary hosts who besiege Caer Arianrhod. Realising she has again been duped, Arianrhod finally condemns him to be wifeless. This difficulty Gwydion also overcomes, making a woman from flowers. Her name 'Blodeuedd' means literally 'Flower Face', but, as the storyteller makes clear, could signify an owl.

After a few years together, Blodeuedd, tiring of her husband, finds a paramour in Goronwy and, with him, plans to free herself by killing Lleu. The difficulty is that he cannot be killed indoors or out of doors, on horse or on foot. Somewhat ingenuously he then explains how the crime may be accomplished. A wash-tub must be prepared by a river bank and covered with a roof of thatch. Next a billy goat must be coaxed to stand beside it. If Lleu then stands with one foot on the tub's edge and the other on the goat's back he will not be indoors or out of doors, on horse or foot and so vulnerable

Blodeuedd tricks him into giving a demonstration and makes all the requisite preparations while Goronwy hides in some bushes. However, the spear he launches turns Lleu into an eagle and with a scream of fury he flies away. The distraught Gwydion searches for him and finally discovers him as an aged and decrepit bird in an oak-tree. He lures him down and with his wand turns him back into human shape. The story ends with the punishment of Blodeuedd and Goronwy.

The next story, 'The Dream of Maxen,' is of late date and is mainly a farrago of patriotic nonsense in which the Welsh beauty Elen (Helen) and her kinsmen supposedly help the Roman emperor Maxentius, who reigned from ad 306 to 312, to regain his lost throne. It ends with an account of how the peninsula forming the north-west corner of France came to be called Brittany.

'Lludd and Llevelys' is more interesting in that it records the foundation of London as Caer Llundein – that is to say, Llud's Castle. As history it is suspect. Llud may possibly survive in names like Ludgate Hill and Ludgate Circus, but the area that is now London was never a Celtic stronghold and other derivations of the name are possible. The rest of the story describes three plagues that beset Llud's people and of the strategems his brother Llevelys, king of France, recommends for ending them.

'The Dream of Rhonabwy,' another of the stories in which Arthur figures, has been dated to the second decade of the thirteenth century and Idris Foster believes it to have been strongly influenced by Geoffrey of Monmouth.

Rhonabwy finds himself in the sordid guest-house belonging to Heilyn the Red and the emphasis the writer puts on the squalor and dirt of the establishment confirms Ammianus Marcellinus's comment about Celtic cleanliness. The hero is compelled to sleep uncomfortably on a flearidden ox-skin and experiences a strange dream full of allusive portents, many of which are indecipherable. The main event is a game of *gwddbwyll* between Arthur and Owein, which goes on while what appears to be a battle between Arthur's men and Owein's ravens is raging. At intervals tired, angry messengers arrive to warn that one side or the other is being pressed and to ask Arthur or Owein to give the necessary orders, requests they both ostentatiously ignore with the remark to their opponent: 'Your move, lord.'

Owein may well be based on the historical figure who was Lord of Rheged in succession to his father Urien, patron of Taliessin and, in another instance of a union between mortal and god, was supposedly born to Modron. She has been equated with Rhiannon, alias Rigatona, the Great Queen, and with the Irish Morrigan, who has another counterpart in the British Morgan le Fay. The Morrigan possesses the power to turn herself into a crow or raven. Thus the ravens, mentioned in the story as being involved in the battle with Arthur's *men,* may actually be Owein's divine mother and her companions (they also feature in the *Tain),* who as battle-maidens have thrown themselves in on his side. On the other hand, Owein is spoken of as having 'a flight of ravens' at the end of the next story, 'Owein, or The Countess of the Fountain,' so it is possible that it refers to some kind of special military unit.

Though the 'Dream' is set in the period in which Arthur was fighting his rearguard battles against the invading Saxons, the idea of visions occurring while the sleeper is lying on an ox-skin is deeply embedded in Celtic thought. The word 'feis,' which came to mean a 'feast,' derives from an Old Irish word meaning 'to sleep with,' but was used to designate the feast at which a new king was symbolically married to the tribe's patron-goddess. This was preceded by the Tarbfeis or ox-dream in which, after the death or removal of one king, the Druids decided which member of the royal clan was to succeed. An ox was sacrificed and all present drank the broth made of its flesh. Then they slept on the skin of the slain animal and, in the dream which came to them, saw who was to be the next king. The Tarbfeis that follows the death of King Eterscel is described in 'The Destruction of Da Derga's Hostel.'

The presence of the ox-skin dream in 'Rhonabwy' suggests the story may originally have been one of those prophecies couched in the elusive metaphor so beloved of the Celts.

The remaining three stories are all of late date, when the original material had been considerably influenced and no doubt recast by the *amour courtoise.*

'The Countess of the Fountain' tells how Owein – he of the 'Dream of Rhonabwy' but here Arthur's boon companion – having heard of Kynon's adventures in the strange land in which he found himself after hurling water from a fountain at a stone, decides to seek it out. Like Kynon, while riding through a deep forest he encounters a black giant by whom he is given directions. When he throws water from the fountain over the stone a furious rainstorm is unleashed, just as had happened with Kynon, and it is followed by exquisite birdsong.

A knight appears and fights him but, mortally wounded, quits the field, pursued by Owein to his castle. Surrounded by enemies, he is, none the less, befriended by Luned, lady-in-waiting of its chatelaine, with whom Owein, espying her in secret, falls instantly in love. Luned undertakes to act as go-between and does so with such success that, despite the fact that the wounded knight dies and Owein has been identified as his killer, the couple wed.

In the meantime, Arthur, pining for Owein's company, organises a search party and, after encounters with the black giant, they find him in his role as defender of the fountain. At the pleading of his friends, Owein returns to the court, promising his wife it will be for no more than three months. However, it is three years later that an angry woman envoy comes to the court to accuse him of betrayal. Remorseful, Owein sets out to find the Castle of the Fountain once more, but fails and instead is called upon to defend another widow-countess from persecution.

After this interlude the story returns to the Countess of the Fountain. Owein comes upon Luned, imprisoned in a stone jar because she has ventured to speak in his defence at her mistress's court. Unaccountably omitting to free her from her uncomfortable prison, at her direction he goes to a castle where he is told food and hospitality is available. Here he gets embroiled in the killing of a giant who has been killing and eating his host's sons, He then goes back to rescue Luned and returns to the realm of the Countess of the Fountain, whom he takes back to Arthur's court as his wife.

In a kind of appendix, Owein kills the Black Oppressor, who has himself killed the husbands-to-be of twenty-four maidens, and returns with the girls to the court where, the storyteller says, Owein served as chief of his lord's retinue 'until he returned to his own land.'

The hero of 'Peredur Son of Evrawg,' the naive, gauche, and supremely innocent country boy, is the prototype of the later Perceval and various attempts have been made to show how the mutation of names might have come about. In fact, Peredur is probably based on an actual figure of that name from Penwddig in north Cardigan.

He of the story is the sole survivor of seven sons, the rest of whom, with their father, have been killed in the wars. Not surprisingly, Peredur's mother is anxious that her son should pursue a less hazardous occupation, but reluctantly bows to the inevitable when, seeing a party of knights, he is overcome by the ambition to become one. She advises him to go to the court of King Arthur, which he does.

He arrives at a moment of crisis. Queen Gwenhwyvar (Guinevere) has just been grossly insulted by an intruder-knight. Then Peredur himself gets embroiled in a quarrel with the surly seneschal Kai, whom he calls 'the tall man.'

Though the story is concerned with Peredur's avenging of the insult to Gwenhwyvar and the resolution of his quarrel with Kai, its main burden is his visit to the courts of the Fisher and the Lame Kings. At the first, he is told that whatever extraordinary sights he sees at the second, he must ask no questions. He obeys these instructions when the bloody spear and the severed head on a platter are borne through the chamber. Later, he is unfairly reproached for failing to ask about these objects, for had he done so the Lame King would have been cured and his land returned to fertility. In fact, we are told that the head is actually that of a slain kinsman whose death it was his duty to avenge.

The last story in the collection, 'Gereint and Enid,' is mainly the description of a series of knightly tourneys, played out against the backdrop of Gereint's unjustified suspicion of his faithful young wife, Enid. Though it is a tale which seems to have undergone the most changes to make it into a fashionable courtly romance, its final scene contains matter plainly very archaic.

Gereint's last battle is with three giants. Already wounded and fatigued from earlier encounters, he overcomes two of them, but only after himself sustaining a serious wound. He falls inert from his horse at the feet of Enid, who utters a scream of horror. This brings on the scene another knight travelling in the vicinity. His name is given as 'Limwris,' a rendering into Welsh of the Old French *li mors*, death.[5]

Limwris believes that Gereint is still alive and takes him to his castle, supposedly to cure him. Once there, however, he makes advances to Enid and, when rebuffed, strikes her. Her second scream brings Gereint to his senses, he immediately lays about the knight and his supporters, defeats them, and leaves with Enid.

Thereafter the story speaks of their travelling 'as if between two hedges' at a time when 'day was giving way to night.' Soon they see spear-shafts against the sky and hear the clamour of a great company. Unsure of their intention, Gereint, who has Enid riding pillion, lifts her over the hedge for safety. A knight turns to pursue, but then identifies himself as 'the Little King' come to help them. He invites them to the nearby court of his brother-in-law where Gereint is treated for his wound. When cured the Little King invites them to his own court.

The journey brings them to a fork in the road. In 'Peredur' the hero encounters a similar situation, though in his case he is presented with a

---

5 It would also be possible to render *Li mors* as 'the bite,' but in this context 'death' seems the more plausible translation.

choice of three roads. Uncertain which way to go, Gereint and his companions ask a traveller who tells them that the one they are on is the better, as the other leads to a place from which none return alive – the court of Earl Owein.

They take the second road, nevertheless, and find it hedged about with mist while within it enchanted games are going on. Ever impulsive, Gereint decides to proceed.

They come to what seems to be a most pleasant spot, are courteously received and lodged at court. Having eaten, they go to where the mysterious games are to take place: the area enshrouded in the hedge of mist. Around it are stakes, each, save two, crowned with a decapitated head. The story does not tell us so, but these must be intended for the heads of Gereint and the Little King.

Gereint alone enters the mist-hedge. Within is an orchard and, in a clearing, a pavilion of red brocade. Outside, a hunting-horn hangs from the branch of an apple-tree.

Gereint dismounts and enters. Its sole occupant is a girl whose golden chair faces another, vacant, one. As Gereint makes for it, she warns him that the owner permits none except himself to sit there. He takes it all the same and a mounted knight at once comes to challenge his right to it. They fight and the challenger is overcome. As the victor is about to behead him the knight cries for mercy, which Gereint promises in return for his abolishing the games and making the mist-hedge and other enchantments disappear.

The knight tells him that to do so Gereint has only to wind the horn hanging from the apple-tree, for it has been prophesied that once a knight who had overcome him did so the mist would vanish and the games come to an end.

The scene is, of course, substantially that described in Chrétien's 'Erec and Enide' and, because of the similarities, it was long believed that one represented a borrowing from the other, though the direction was disputed. This has now given place to the belief that both more probably derived from a common source. The evidence for this includes numerous names in the Chrétien version, many of them of Welsh ancestry.

Also to be counted among the British Matter is, of course, 'Tristan and Isolt.' The oldest version in our possession, that of Beroul, is incomplete, starting well on into the story, but there is no reason to believe that Joseph Bedier's completion is too wide of the mark.

The plot is extremely complicated, with all the elements not only of romance but of high drama. Tristan, a young knight at the court of King Mark (March) of Cornwall, is, though the king does not know it, his nephew He defends his liege-lord's right not to pay tribute-money to the Irish and, though he mortally wounds his adversary, the champion

Morholt, he leaves a shard of his own sword blade buried in his skull and is himself badly wounded. His injuries refuse to heal and he is sent to Ireland to be nursed by the healing hand of Isolt, daughter of the High King of Ireland and Morholt's niece. However, Isolt has preserved the shard left in her uncle's skull and sworn vengeance on his killer.

Back in Cornwall, Tristan sings the praises of Isolt to the wifeless Mark, who decides to marry her, and Tristan returns to Ireland to escort her, walking into the trap awaiting him. But the country is being ravaged by a dragon so ferocious that the king has promised Isolt's hand to any who can slay him. Though he succeeds, Tristan is overcome by the dragon's poison and as he lies unconscious, a seneschal claims to have been the dragon's slayer and demands the hand of an unwilling Isolt. She discovers Tristan's comatose body, however, and realises that he is the true dragon-killer.[6] While he is lying in a curative bath, Isolt sees that his sword has a nick in the blade. Secretly comparing it with the shard in her keeping she finds it fits perfectly, but she has to spare his life since it is her sole means of escaping marriage to the seneschal. Instead of claiming Isolt for himself, Tristan claims her as bride of his uncle.

On the return journey the couple accidentally swallow a love-potion prepared for her daughter and future son-in-law by Isolt's mother. They fall hopelessly in love and it is their illicit, but inadvertent, liaison which forms the burden of Beroul's story and in which the correspondences with the Irish 'Grainme' story are most apparent. Though Mark's suspicions are repeatedly aroused, the couple are able to allay them, until a trail of blood from a cut Tristan has sustained leads from his bed to the queen's. The couple manage to escape, but are condemned to death in absentia.

After various attempts to hunt them down – a further echo of 'Grainme' – when they are finally successful, Isolt is able to prove her innocence, partly by the intercession of Gawain (Gwalchmei) who has been despatched by King Arthur as intermediary, and is restored to the king. Tristan goes to Brittany and there marries another Isolt, she of the White Hand, not because he loves her, but because of her passion for him. Wounded in battle, he is advised that only Isolt of Ireland can cure him, and she is accordingly sent for. Before leaving Brittany, the courier is directed to fly white sails on his return journey if she is with him, black is she not.

When the returning vessel is sighted, Tristan asks his wife the colour of its sails. She, out of jealousy, replies that they are black and Tristan dies. Isolt of Ireland, expires from grief.

The influence of the continental *amour courtoise* tradition is evident and the love-potion can only have been introduced to make Tristan and

---

6 The dragon-slaying and false claimant is a motif which occurs throughout the Celtic lands, including Jersey where a pair of chapels built on top of the burial mound at La Hougue Bie are said to commemorate just such an event.

Isolt's love appear innocent to Christian eyes. Nonetheless, there is much that is archaic in the story, even in its surviving form: in Tristan's and Mark's rivalry for Isolt, as in Diarmait's and Finns for Grainme, Kulhwch's and Ysbaddaden's for Olwen, or, come to that, Lancelot's and Arthur's for Guinevere. There is also the theme of a young suitor as rival to an older one, the significance of which will be discussed later.

One of the characters in 'Tristan and Isolt,' the dwarf Frocin, is plainly a Druid. He alone knows the secret of King Mark's horse-ears – yet another similarity to the Irish King Labhraidh Lorc where a Druid is also involved in uncovering the secret. (In an astonishing parallel with modern teaching, Druidism held that the 'repression' of such things was psychologically harmful.) In other words, however tortuous its route of transmission 'Tristan and Isolt' obviously belongs to the Celtic myth canon.

THE TOPOGRAPHY
OF A
SUPERNATURAL WORLD

Chapter 7

DRUIDISM

Even making maximum allowance for cross-fertilisation and reciprocal borrowing, the Matters of Ireland and Britain show sufficient correspondences to prove that both came from what had once been a common source.

Nowhere are these more marked than in two poems, one by Amergin from *The Yellow Book of Lecan* and the second from Taliessin's 'The Battle of the Trees.' Amergin speaks of himself as being the wind, a wave, a murmur of the billows, a bull, a vulture, a sun ray, a plant, a wild boar, a salmon, a lake, the craft of the artificer, the word of science, the spearpoint that gives battle. Taliessin goes through a similar list in which he says he was a he-goat, a sage plant, a boar, a horn, a wild sow, a shout in battle, a stream on the slope, a wave on the shore, the gleam of a downpour, a tabby-headed cat on three trees, a ball, a head, a well-fed crane.

Though several items in each poem are the same, what is important is neither this nor the fact that several of those mentioned – the bull, the boar, the salmon, the cat, the crane – are known cult creatures. It is actually the differences that are instructive, for if one had merely copied from the other both lists would have been substantially the same. Similarity of form with difference of content suggests a single poetic heritage.

But as well as parallels of this kind we have those of detail within the stories. For example, the Connaught hero Fergus has a magic sword, *Caladcholg*, obviously the counterpart of Arthur's sword called in the *Mabinogion* 'Caledvwlch.' The ritual game of *fidchell* is *gwddbwyll* in Britain. Finnabair, daughter of Mebd and Ailill, is the counterpart of Guinevere. There are numerous, slightly changed god-names, so that the Irish Danu becomes the British Don, and Goibniu, Govannon. Llud is the British equivalent of the Irish Nuada of the Silver Hand (in 'Kulhwch and Olwen' he is called 'Ludd of the Silver Hand'), and the Macha of the Irish stories appears as Rhiannon in the British Matter. There are also common themes, such as the conflict between a younger man and an older one for the love of a woman.

At the same time, the considerable differences cannot be ignored. The picture that emerges from the Irish Matter is of a vigorous, passionate people, of men remorseless in the protection of honour, given to self-adornment and almost childish bombast, fatalistically ruled by their *gessa* so that Cu Chulainn dies when he eats dog; King Conare, bird-meat. Their principal activities are fighting and feasting accompanied by drinking so excessive that quarrels ending in bloody brawls are commonplace.

Less of this primitive dynamism has survived in the British Matter. Single combats, even entire wars, are recorded in a sentence or two, where an Irish storyteller would have lingered over them. Men court women and frequently end up, like Pwyll and Rhiannon, spending 'nights in pleasure and delight.' Yet, though we are assured that this or that woman was the 'loveliest in the world,' her charms – her foxglove cheek, long yellow hair, Parthian-red lips, her white pointed breasts – are seldom enumerated. We know little of what she wore or how it became her. Least of all are there the dire warnings against the perils that flow from beauty, of the 'heavy harvest of fighting men' it can provoke.

These divergences between the two traditions can be accounted for in a number of ways. Local patriotism would be one. It could well have been this which led Britons to substitute for the Irish account of Lugh's genesis as a god of the Tuatha one making him their own kinsman. There were, besides, different economies: Britain was a land of cereal growing; the Irish bred cattle and horses. Most of all there was the separation which had taken place in the language.

What is less easy to account for is the presence in the British Matter, of so much that is eerily fantastic and magical and whose origins can only be Druidic. On the face of it one would have expected the reverse. The British Druids were under Roman prohibition; in Ireland, they had survived apparently unmolested until the arrival of the first Christian missionaries. Part of the answer to this may lie in Caesar's statement that Britain was regarded as the place where Druidism began and to which all who wanted to advance their studies in the subject repaired. In Stuart Piggott's opinion the assertion has substance. The Irish myths mention a Druid returning from his studies in Britain and archaeologists have found signs that practices such as shaft burial that long predated the Celts' arrival in Britain continued after it, as if they had taken over whatever religion they had found in situ. It had, of course, produced some stunningly impressive monuments in the stone circles and henges of which Avebury and Stonehenge were spectacular examples. Whatever the purpose of these, it may well have been that the Druids continued to maintain them as ritual centres, making the country the home of many of their most important sacred sites.

Another part of the answer may be connected with my suggestion in Chapter 3 that the British Druids eluded Roman persecution by passing themselves off as bards. Even when so disguised they could be expected to preserve the doctrinal element in their stories.

Yet another may actually be the result of that persecution itself. Some scholars see, in the period leading up to the conquest, signs of an emerging Celtic nationhood with the Druids as its focus, and advance the desire to thwart it at all costs as the motive for the Roman invasion. There is, in fact, no evidence of any such element in Roman reasoning and, in my view, such evidence as we have actually suggests Druidic influence in Celtic society might have been waning.

Some of this evidence comes from Ireland. Once Druids themselves, it was not surprising that, having become established as a body of professional storytellers, the *filid* would be more interested in the literary than the religious content of their repertoire. All the same, Druids were not, one would have thought, lightly to be made into figures of fun, particularly since ridicule was the thing the Celts most detested. Yet this is how the Druids Cromm Deroil and Cromm Daril, 'foster-sons of the most excellent Cathbad', are portrayed in 'The Intoxication of the Ulstermen.'

In Britain, by persecuting the Druids the Romans could well have done what persecution so often does – given its victims a fresh lease on life, and all the more so when Druidism alone must have represented to the minds of most ordinary people their own past independence and, perhaps, the hope of its future return.

However, this is not to imply that Druidic elements are absent from the Irish tales, Great Druids like Cathbad, Fer Rogain, mac Roth and Uath mac Imoman appear and retain such magical powers as shape-shifting, levitation, prophecy, healing, and clairvoyance.

Furthermore, the very nature of the Irish Matter makes it clear that it is, at root, hierophany or sacred history. Invariably this records events in the history of a people and in the lives of their heroes in a way which emphasises the special regard in which they are held by the divine. An obvious example is the Old Testament, in which the entire history of the Jewish people and the lives of heroes like Joshua are shown as flowing out of the favour with Yahweh. In the same way, Cu Chulainn, for instance, is under the special protection of Lugh.

Since the reverberations of Druidism are so clearly audible, a knowledge of it ought to provide us with a most valuable key to decoding the myths. Sadly, information is sketchy and unreliable

The only statement of Druidic doctrine, contained in the two-volume *Barddas* compiled by the sixteenth-century Llewellyn Sion of Glamorgan, describes a dualistic philosophy in which God represents the creative, life-endowing energies and Cythrawl those of destruction and annihilation. To begin with there existed only Annwn, the Abyss, but organic life began when God called from it the primal substance Manred. Manred was made up of indivisible particles or atoms, each a divine microcosm. As the source of life, the Abyss now becomes 'Abred.'

It is presumably with the coming of life that Cythrawl enters the picture though we are not told precisely how this happened.

Schematically, the universe is presented as a trio of concentric circles with Abred, the source of life, as the innermost. All living things pass through it and, during their sojourn, experience every form of existence and suffer every sort of hardship, before ascending to the next circle that of Gwynfyd (= Purity), which the evolving soul enters when once it has qualified for membership of the human race. The last circle is that of Ceugant or Infinity inhabited by God alone, but apparently somewhat similar to the Buddhist Nirvana and the Hindu Brahma in that the soul that attains it merges with the divine

Some of the details given in the *Barddas* accord with what we know of Druidism. Three, the number of the concentric circles, was sacred to the Druids, while the dualistic character of the *Barddas* system might help to explain why Pliny brackets Druidism with Persian Magianism, which was also dualistic.

However, these cannot be taken as evidence for the authenticity of the *Barddas*. Anyone attempting to reconstruct Druidic doctrines would obviously incorporate what was known of them and, as a whole, the work is regarded with suspicion. Anachronistic Christian figures and events appear and many of its ideas can be traced to the fashionable Neoplatonism of the author's time. What is more, there is a complete absence of any confirmatory hint in the mythology.

The *Barddas* dismissed, we are left with only three sources: (1) a handful of classical literary references; (2) archaeological data; and (3) such knowledge as can be gathered from drawing analogies between the Celtic and other societies either at a similar developmental level or with which they are known to have been associated.

Of the first, works on the Celts by Aristotle and Timagenes, dating to the fourth and first centuries BC respectively and thus written at a time when first-hand observation was possible, are now entirely lost except for some quotations in other writers. A book by Posidonius, who must have travelled in the Celtic lands, as he was said to have been nauseated by the sight of warriors carrying wreaths of heads from the battlefield, and who wrote in the second century BC, is known only from the citations in Diodorus of Sicily (c. 40 BC) and Strabo (63 BC–AD 21).

From the latter we learn of other customs connected with the head, such as that of embalming particularly valued ones in cedar oil to show off as proof of martial prowess. In other cases, they were mounted on spikes above houses or set in door-lintels. Skulls were sometimes converted into drinking cups and the Roman historian Titus Livy describes a gold-mounted one used for such a purpose

The much-quoted description of Druidism in *The Conquest of Gaul* was written, not by Caesar but by his friend Hirtius and was ultimately

Figure 1: The Gundestrup Cauldron (*Danish National Museum, Copenhagen*).

Figure 2: The horned god Cernunnos shown on the interior of a ceremonial cauldron found in a bog at Gundestrup in Denmark. This artefact, provisionally dated to about 100 BC, shows him surrounded by animals and holding the Celtic torc in his right hand while in his left he grasps a ram-headed serpent (*Danish National Museum, Copenhagen*).

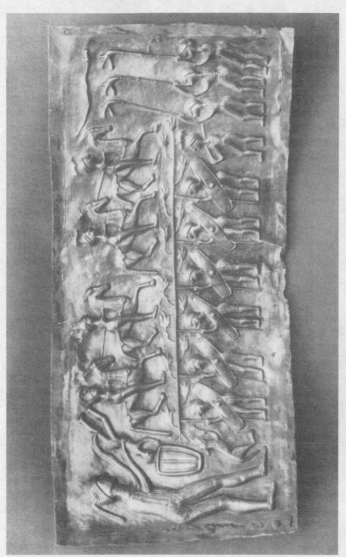

Figure 3: Frieze of warriors from the Gundestrup Cauldron (*Danish National Museum, Copenhagen*).

Figure 4: The Aylesford Bucket. This splendid artifact in the La Tene style was found among grave-goods in a Belgic cemetery at Aylesford, Kent. Made of wooden staves bound with bronze bands its decoration includes representations of gods and stylised horses (*British Museum*).

Figure 5: A typical example of one of the magnificent torcs which have been found all over the Celtic cultural province. Though their exact significance is unknown, it was plainly ritualistic as the torc is represented in most Celtic art, including the Gundestrup Cauldron where the figure of the horned-god Cernunnos is shown wearing one and holding another in his right hand (*British Museum*).

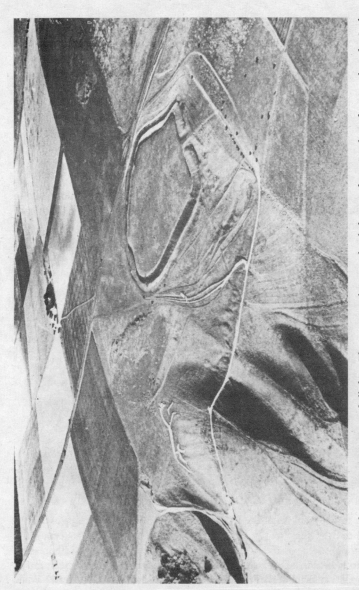

Figure 6: A characteristic iron-age hill-fort. These not only served a defensive function but, from archaeological evidence, also provided facilities for the storage of such commodities as corn (*Ashmolean Museum, Oxford*).

Figure 7: A stone head from Gloucester. The head played a crucial role in Druidic belief and among Celtic customs was that of beheading fallen enemies and preserving or displaying the heads outside their homes (*Gloucester City Museum and Art Gallery*).

Figure 8: The survival of the Druidic cult of water sources, supposedly an access to the Other World. Here a representation of a Biblical scene—the finding of Moses—made from leaves forms part of an annual well dressing ceremony held in a Derbyshire village. Similar ceremonies can be found in other parts of Britain, while the numerous Bridewells and St. Anne's Wells to be found all over the country are certainly the survivals of two important Druidic deities—Brigid and Anu (*British Tourist Authority*).

Figure 9: The Abbotts Bromley 'stag men' in Staffordshire—another local festival which recalls the Druidic deities, in this case Cernunnos, the horned god. Carbon dating of the antlers has shown at least one span to date back to pre-Norman times. A religious festival held in Brittany, in honour of 'St. Cornely,' patron-saint of horned animals, probably commemorates the same deity and it is significant that both occasions take place in the early days of September each year (*British Tourist Authority*).

Figure 10: 'Gorsedd of the Bards of Kernow' in Cornwall—despite the strong Celtic links to be found on the peninsula, this ceremony owes more to imagination than history (*British Tourist Authority*).

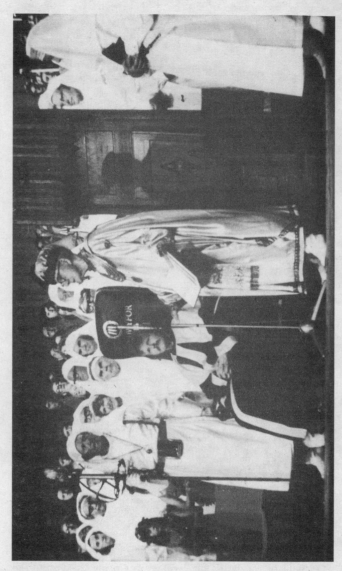

Figure 11: The crowning of the 'Archdruid' at the Welsh Eisteddfod. Such colourful rituals, dating from about the 19th century, are completely without historical sanction, although there was a link between the Druids and the Bards (*Wales Tourist Board*).

derived from Posidonius, for which reason much of its information may well have been out-of-date. Besides, in order to justify his military adventures, Caesar needed to present Druidism in the most unfavourable light possible and so would have used his sources selectively (Posidonius, on the whole, admired the Celts). Nonetheless, it is the fullest account we have. From it we learn that the Druids were teachers, law-givers, and interpreters of religious questions. They were responsible for the regulation of worship and sacrifice and the book describes a form in which a wickerwork giant was filled with victims and burnt. Although the sufferers were in general condemned criminals, the author adds that if insufficient were available they did not scruple to pack their manikin with the innocent.

He tells us that the Druids had the power to ban individuals and even tribes from attendance at the sacrifice, the worst punishment that could be inflicted. The fact they could ban 'whole tribes' helps to corroborate other evidence that the Druids possessed powers which went beyond the purely tribal and that they were, in fact, 'pan-tribal.'

The sacrifices to which Caesar refers are mainly those which took place at the four yearly festivals: Samain, the Celtic new year (approximating to Hallowe'en), Beltaine, the year's mid point, corresponding to our own May Day; Imbolc, the lactation of the ewes in February; and Lugnasad, connected with the corn harvest in August. However he also mentions what appears to be a form of propitiatory sacrifice in which another human life was offered to save that of someone who was sick. This implies a Druidic belief in cosmic balance which, as we shall see, is borne out elsewhere. Among other Druidic beliefs he singles out reincarnation.

He further tells us that Druidic studies took twenty years, that all teaching was oral, and he describes an annual convention of the Gaulish Druids which took place at a consecrated place in the territory of the Carnutes, supposedly the centre of the country. This coincides approximately with the Beauce, the region of north-west France stretching south-west of Paris toward the Forest of Orleans and includes Chartres. Since Christian edifices were usually erected on or near sites of significance to paganism, their size and magnificence being a measure of the awe in which a site was formerly held, the presence at Chartres of the finest Gothic cathedral in Europe may pinpoint it as Caesar's 'consecrated place.'

Another Roman writer, Pliny the Elder, in his *Natural History* describes a mistletoe-gathering ceremony, thereby giving licence for the white robes worn by the Druids' later emulators, though there is nothing to show these formed their normal costume.

Cicero, Caesar's contemporary and one-time friend, met Diviciacus, chief of the Aeduan tribe, who may also have been a Druid. He was obviously impressed by him and speaks of the Druids as possessing that knowledge 'the Greeks call "Physiologia"'; but Cicero had studied at the Athenian

Academy whose philosophy in his time was predominantly Stoic and may have been carried away by their enthusiasm for 'the Noble Savage.' He had, besides, visited another eminent Stoic, none other than Posidonius, at his home in Rhodes.

The Roman poet Lucan (AD 39–65) mentions the Druids in his *Pharsalia* as having their abode in the 'innermost groves of far-off forests' and may well have heard or even seen the Druidic grove near the Greek trading-post at Massilia. He mentions the belief in reincarnation and, like Caesar, credits it with imbuing the Celts with great courage in war. He also speaks with considerable distaste of human sacrifice.

This is again singled out by Tacitus who, in his eulogising account of the Roman seizure of Mon (Anglesey), speaks of the Druids as deeming it 'a duty to cover their altars with the blood of captives and to consult their deities through human entrails.'

Unfortunately, our second potential witness, archaeology, has so far produced little which can be confidently assigned to Druidism and some of the archaeological record is, at best, ambiguous. A case in point are the animal forms, often highly stylised, found on numerous Celtic artefacts. The fact that some – such as the fish, the horse, the stag, the boar, the bull, the eagle, the swan and other birds – recur in the myths would, on its own, suggest a cult significance. On the other hand, many of them must be purely decorative.

What archaeology does provide is a list of 374 god-names of which 305 have been found only once, while of the remaining sixty-nine the number occurring from twenty to thirty times is fewer than ten. This is at odds with other accounts. Caesar lists six gods, which he says were those most worshipped in Gaul. They are: Mercury, Apollo, Mars, Jupiter, and Minerva, as well as Dispater, from whom, he said, all Gauls claimed descent. Despite his use of Roman names, several lists of equivalents have been assembled. The most commonly agreed one gives Lugh for Mercury, Belinus/Beli for Apollo, Taranis for Mars, Teutatis for Jupiter, Brigid for Minerva and Cernunnos for Dispater, but this is far from universally accepted and, indeed, in Gallo-Roman times the occupiers frequently confused the issue by attaching the names of one of their own gods to several different Celtic ones, so that, for example, the name of the war god Mars is found, not only on dedications to Taranis, but to Cocidius, Rudiobus, Teutatis, and Loucetius, while in others Belenos, Lugh, and Maponus are all equated with Apollo.

The medieval Berne *Scholiasts,* who annotated Lucan's *Pharsalia,* name three gods: Esus, Teutatis, and Taranis, all of whom do in fact occur in epigraphy. Others archaeologically attested over a wide area are Nodens, Lugus, Belenos, and Cernunnos. Feminine deities include the horse goddess Epona and Ireland has In Dagda, the good god ('good,' that is to say, in the diversity of his talents rather than in his moral character).

Professor Anne Ross explains the discrepancy between the profusion of god-names known to archaeology and the small number named by Caesar and others as due to the fact that this select group were members of an all-Celtic pantheon which the Druids were in the process of promoting. But, of course, there may always have been a body of what might be called national deities invoked side by side with the purely tribal ones, especially since Druidism itself had a notably 'national' character.

There were probably other factors, however. The Celts' were markedly reluctant to utter the true names of gods, presumably because if known by enemies they, too, might invoke them. 'I swear by the gods by whom my people swear' is a formula repeatedly found in the myths. An alternative way of avoiding enunciation of the name was to use an epithet. These, appearing on dedications, have been assumed to be names, so that Segomo, 'The Mighty One,' Rigisamus, and 'The Most Kingly' have been taken as the names for separate gods when they may simply be descriptives, just as the Greeks might call Apollo 'Phoebus,' the enlightener, or 'Hecatebolos,' the far-shooter.

But another reason for the large number was the practice of attaching several names to one deity. The sinister Other World woman who enters Da Derga's Hostel while Conare is there introduces herself as Cailb. When Conare jests at its brevity she tells him: 'Indeed, I have many other names' and proceeds to rattle off more than thirty. The Irish Lugh, who figures in the British Matter as Lleu, has been equated with the Irish Finn, with Pryderi and even Gawain, while Tolstoy equates him with Mabon, 'The Young Son' who appears in Ireland as Oengus mac Oc. With replication of this kind it would not be difficult to reach the nearly 400 god names so far discovered.

What archaeology does provide, however, is concrete evidence of at least some Celtic customs.

One is that of decapitation. A sanctuary at Rocquepertuse in France has niches for several heads, some still with skulls in them, incorporated into the stonework and similar discoveries have been made at other sites, including British ones. (This may be the origin of the custom of using representations of human heads as features in architectural decoration, one more commonly found in the Celtic lands than elsewhere.)

Consistent with what we know of Druidism are the open enclosures, surrounded by a palisade or ditch, occurring in many parts of the Celtic culture-province. In a number of places shafts containing pottery, bones, and carved figures have been found, such as the one discovered in the autumn of 1984 in a site near Deal in Kent. Some, though not all, of these shafts may once have been wells and this would be consistent with the Druidic belief in an Underworld accessible through water, further confirmed by Strabo's reference to gold and silver bullion found in and by a lake near Toulouse and the finds of treasure such as that at La Tène in Switzerland and Llyn Cerrig Bach in Anglesey.

The so-called Coligny calendar picked up by a roadside near Bourg-en-Bresse in the last century and thought to date from the first century BC shows the Druids to have been calendarists who reconciled lunar and solar years by means of a nineteen-year or Metonic cycle.

But indisputably the most informative of all the archaeological data is the great cauldron from Gundestrup in Denmark. There are many references to cauldrons in the myths and the sacerdotal purpose of the one from Gundestrup is beyond doubt, for on its panels are representations of gods, often with their attributes, among them the horned Cernunnos seated in the Buddha-like, cross-legged pose we know the Celts to have employed.

Another panel shows a large figure grasping by the ankles a much smaller one, whom he is about to immerse head first in a cauldron or, as some authorities have it, the opening of a ritual shaft. It is usually taken to be a scene of human sacrifice, drowning having been one of the methods used. However, it is another example of how archaelogical material is often open to more than one interpretation. In the myths we have references to warriors being restored to life after passing through a magic cauldron and Jean Markale believes that this is what is portrayed here.

Other archaeological data includes an oak coffin exhumed from a tumulus at Grisethorpe, near Scarborough, in 1834 containing the skeleton of an old man. The coffin was covered with oak branches and within were the remains of foliage identified at the time as mistletoe. Tumulus burial accords with known custom and the presence of mistletoe in this, taken with Pliny's description of the mistletoe-culling ceremony, looks like substantive proof of origin, especially now that mistletoe pollen has been found in the gut of Lindow Man, the Iron Age body found in a peat-bog at Lindow Moss near Wilmslow, Cheshire, in 1984. Unfortunately, doubts surrounding the rest of the Grisethorpe discovery extend to the nature of the foliage.

The last item on the list of the archaeological data putatively ascribable to the Druids is a 4-foot high sandstone slab found at Port St. Mary in the Isle of Man. It is dated to the fifth or sixth centuries AD and carries an inscription in Ogham, a form of runic script, which has been read as, 'Dovaidona Maqi Droata' – Dovaidona son of the Druid.

Much of what we have from these sources is reflected and, in some cases, amplified in the mythology. For example, Lucan's reference to the Druids as having 'their abodes in far off forests' is mirrored in 'Bricriu's Feast' where the Druid Uath mac Imoman lives by a remote lake. Those 'hermits' so frequently encountered by knights-errant of the Arthurian stories are, as Markale points out, certainly Druids christianised by later storytellers, while according to early accounts the figure taken to be the prototype for Merlin is said to have lived in the wild.

The cauldron, of which that from Gundestrup is such an impressive example, is a repeated myth-motif, indicating its importance as a cult-object. Most obviously it brings to mind the gold cauldron discovered by Pryderi in 'Manwydan,' but the many others mentioned include the cauldron of Diwrnach, one of the objects which Kulhwch and his companions have to deliver to Ysbaddaden before he will permit Olwen to marry. This must be the cauldron of Tyrnoc referred to in 'The Thirteen Treasures of the Island of Britain' and in Taliessin's poem 'The Spoils of Annwyn.' In both instances it has to be brought from Ireland and the dangerous expeditions mounted for the purpose are justified by its marvellous character for, while it will boil the meat of the brave instantly, it refuses to cook that of cowards. The fact that it comes from Ireland recalls the cauldron of the Irish Dagda, which fed all 'save cowards or deceivers,' from which 'no company departed without being grateful to it,' and which had, besides, the capacity of restoring the dead to life.

Taliessin is himself associated with the cauldron of Cerridwen. During a former existence as Gwyon Bach he is set to watch over it as it brews the magic potion that is to provide Cerridwen's hideous son with compensatory wisdom. When a splash of hot liquid lands on one of Gwyon's fingers he spontaneously puts it to his mouth, thereby acquiring the wisdom himself as well as incurring Cerridwen's wrath. A similar accident befalls the Irish Finn while he is cooking the salmon of knowledge for his Druidmaster, Finegal.

The property of restoring life possessed by the Dagda's cauldron is shared by that of Bran who tells King Mallolwch of Ireland, to whom he gives it in compensation for an insult offered him in Britain, that if a man who has been slain is thrown into it he will arise on the morrow as well as ever, except he will have lost the power of speech. Later in the tale its efficacy is tested and proved. The resurrection-theme recurs in 'Peredur.' While visiting the court of the sons of the King of Sufferings, three corpses slain by a dragon are brought in. Women of the court wash each of them in an enormous tub of warm water, whence they emerge restored to life.

This capacity may connect these cauldrons with the belief of reincarnation of which both Caesar and Lucan speak, and some commentators have also seen evidence for this in the poems of Taliessin and Amergin quoted at the beginning of this chapter. However, it is one thing to be reborn as a bird, animal, insect and plant, and quite another for Taliessin and Amergin to claim that they were reincarnated as 'the murmur of the billows,' a 'sun ray,' 'the craft of the artificer,' or 'the spearpoint.'

More convincing testimony of the belief lies elsewhere. The sixth-century Irish abbot St. Finnen befriended Tuan mac Cairill who, at the saint's bidding, was prevailed upon to recite the history of Ireland. It soon becomes clear that Tuan believes himself to have lived through all the events he is describing. First he is a man who 'sat in the assembly that gave the judgments of Partholon,' subsequently he is reborn as a stag, a boar, and finally as a salmon, which is eaten by Cairill, the wife of a chieftain, and passes into her womb for him to be reborn as Tuan.

Very similar is the *Hanes Taliessin,* another work by the British bard, in which, among other epiphanies, the poet speaks of having been a hoplite in the army of Alexander the Great, of being in Canaan when Absalom died, and at the Court of Don before the birth of Gwydion.[7]

What might be called potential rather than actual reincarnation, in which a hero is said to lie 'sleeping' in some secret place awaiting his country's call, is associated with Arthur and Finn. The concept is undoubtedly archaic, for in Greek myth the Titan Kronus, successor of Uranus and predecessor of Zeus, is said to lie sleeping with his retinue ultimately to reawaken. Plutarch (AD 46 – 120) locates his bed-chamber in an island near Britain.

While the myths have no direct references to human sacrifice, 'The Intoxication of the Ulstermen' and two of the Irish 'Destruction' tales – 'Dind Rig' and 'Da Derga's Hostel' – have passages hinting at it. All take place at Samain, when sacrifice is known to have been offered, and contain references to the burning down of a building.

The last motif recurs in 'Branwen daughter of Llyr,' where the victims are the giant Llassar Laes Gyngwyd and his wife, who had earlier stepped from a lake bearing a huge cauldron. When they become increasingly ill-disposed towards those who have given them sanctuary their destruction is encompassed. They are trapped in an iron house which is made white hot, but they manage to break out and escape. This has prompted some writers to see in it the same cryptic hints as are contained in the three Irish stories. In fact, there may be another explanation. A passing reference to Llassar Laes Gyngwyd in 'Manawydan' associates him with saddlery and enamelling. The latter, which was a Celtic invention, requires very high temperatures to liquefy the glass used in it so that the 'iron-house' in 'Branwen' could well represent an enameller's kiln.

There is little doubt that Druidic sacrifice included the Triple Death mentioned by Lucan. Usually this involved hanging or strangulation, fol-

---

7 Don is the British form of the Irish Dana, *déesse-fondatrice* of the Tuatha De Danann, but 'The Court of Dana' is also the Celtic name for the constellation of Cassiopeia.

lowed by burning or stabbing and immersion in water. At least one king, Muirchertach mac Erca, is known to have died in this way and Lindow Man, who if not a king was certainly an aristocrat, underwent such a death. Post-mortem examination shows that he was first stunned with two blows from an axe, then garrotted with a ligature so tight that it broke his neck. Finally, his throat was cut. It has been suggested that this was to let the blood flow, but there can, of course, have been no blood flow after death as circulation would have ceased, though the custom of cutting the throats of victims to allow this to happen – presumably as a ritual fertilisation of the earth – is known from other contexts.

Tolstoy suggests that the death of Lleu described in 'Math son of Mathonwy,' in which he is stabbed with a spear while standing with one foot on a bath of water placed on a river's bank, may also contain relics of a Triple Death. The same writer discusses a reference to it in a manuscript in the British Library which refers to Merlin's being pierced with a stake, stoned, and then drowned.

The practice akin to sacrifice of severing and preserving the head, of which both the classical sources and archaeology give testimony, repeatedly occurs in both Irish and British Matters. We are told that King Conchobhar of Ulster had a room full of these trophies and they also figure in 'Gereint' and 'Peredur.'

The practice survives even in versions as late as Malory's *Morte d'Arthur* (fifteenth century). In Chapter 25 of Book VIII, Sir Tristram, a prisoner of Sir Breunor at the castle of Pluere, is told of a custom whereby Sir Breunor's lady and his own travelling companion, 'La Beale Isoud,' will be judged as to their beauty and whoever is deemed the less fair beheaded. Isoud wins the contest and Tristram – not without expressing disgust – strikes off the head of Sir Breunor's mistress. This is not the end of the affair, however, for he now has to fight Sir Breunor himself and whoever is defeated must forfeit his head. Tristram succeeds in 'thrusting Sir Breunor down grovelling,' unlaces his helm and beheads him.

Apart from its probable Scythic origin, the rationale behind the custom is uncertain. No doubt the Celts, like most ancient peoples, believed the soul to be located in the skull so that the possession of an enemy's head might seem to be a means of insuring against his wrath. But as an explanation of the practice it is incomplete and does not, for example, account for wonder-working heads like those of Bran or of Cu Chualainn's father, Sualdam, which continues to call the Ulstermen to arms after separation from his body.

The dim outlines of a possible ritual significance can just be made out in Chrétien's 'Lancelot.' About to spare the life of a defeated enemy, a ragged and bare-headed woman arrives on a mule and begs Lancelot to cut off and give her the man's head. Reluctantly the hero agrees to renew combat and again is victorious. He now fulfils the Maid of the Mule's petition, and she, full of gratitude, goes off with her bleeding prize. Her unkempt state identifies her as an Other World woman for, like those contorted, hump-backed and often one-eyed males who figure in other stories, it is thus that the immortals often choose to reveal themselves to mortals; but the reasons for her pressing request remain unexplained.

Among the various gods, Lleu/Lugh, Caesar's Mercury, is repeatedly encountered in the myths, supporting the statement that he was 'the god most venerated in Gaul.' Nodens, known from Continental iconography, is the Nuada/Llud. Belinus is probably the Beli the Great mentioned in 'Branwen daughter of Llyr,' 'Manawydan,' 'The Dream of Maxen,' and 'Llud and Lleveylys.' Macha of the Irish stories and the Rhiannon of the British are both usually equated with the continental Epona.

Professor Ross believes the horned-god Cernunnos to be the character designated as Conall Cernach in several of the Irish epics. In evidence she offers not only the horn-element, Cern- in both names, but the fact that in the 'Tain Bo Froech' (The Cattle Raid of Froech) Conall Cernach overcomes a snake. This is precisely what the Cernunnos of the Gundestrup Cauldron appears to be doing. He is also recognizable as the 'black giant' in 'Owein,' where he is described as being surrounded by the animals of the forest whom he rules as lord. Once again the Gundestrup panel provides evidence, for it shows Cernunnos among animals.[8]

---

8   He is almost certainly commemorated in 'Herne the Hunter,' said to haunt, among other places Windsor Great Park, and who figures in Shakespeare's *The Merry Wives of Windsor*.

Chapter 8

NEIGHBOURS, FOREFATHERS, AND COUSINS

From the sources so far examined the Druids emerge as a body which, whatever decline it underwent in later years, was in its heyday the most powerful in Celtic society. Besides explicit testimony to this effect from foreign observers, we can deduce as much from Caesar's assertion that they could ban entire tribes from sacrifice, from their freedom to cross all boundaries, and from the ability mentioned by Strabo and Diodorus of intervening in wars to keep opposing sides apart. The Druids described by Tacitus at the Battle of Anglesey well may have been attempting something of the kind and seem to have been partially successful for, according to the writer, it took all the coercion of the Roman officers to make their men advance. Their power is reflected in the myths. For example, in the Tain Bo Cuailnge we are told that even the Ulster king never spoke before his Druids had first done so.

After a long apprenticeship – in which all teaching was oral – the Druids served their society as healers, prophets, teachers and law-givers, though their main responsibility was the promulgation of doctrine and the governance of religious observance. The latter included the worship of deities, some of whom occur in lists such as Caesar's, in the epigraphy and, in a number of instances, in the myths. Central to their worship was the dedication of human offerings.

The third source of information mentioned in the last chapter – comparison between the Celts and those peoples who had been their neighbours or who came from the same racial stock – is, naturally enough, one that must be used with caution and without abandoning oneself to the temptation to extrapolate freely, even where analogies seem most obvious. Nonetheless, such parallels as can safety be drawn may help to set Druidism into a context.

We saw earlier how greatly the Celts were influenced by the Scythians. Among the Scythians mediation with the supernatural was the function of the Enarees, a word meaning roughly 'menwomen.' The Enarees spoke in high-pitched voices and wore female attire, the change of sex being held to be their punishment for the desecration of the temple of a goddess. They may have been eunuchs, but this is neither certain nor inevitable. There is, of course, no suggestion that the Druids ever surrendered their masculinity in any way, though one cannot help wondering whether 'The Labour Pains of the Ulstermen' does not conceal some kind of hidden message.

The Enarees served their community as healers, prophets, teachers and law-givers and, like the Druids, were credited with the ability to change shape, using for the purpose a magic wand. As its material, they appear to have favoured willow, while the Druids, according to Markale, chose yew and mountain-ash. However, it is probable that they also used hazel as the tree associated with wisdom in Celtic lore and out of which the traditional water-diviner's rod was made.

The Scythians exerted other influences, too. The metre-high cauldron, now in the Hermitage Museum in Leningrad, recalls those found on Celtic sites. Its owners practised drowning-sacrifice – the Leningrad cauldron may have served such a purpose – perhaps explaining the scene on the Gundestrup Cauldron as well as its actual function.

Inflicting death by such means accords with the Celtic preoccupation with water and water-sources as the dwelling-place of supernatural entities, a motif also found in the myths. Merlin is repeatedly connected with water. The Druid Uath mac Imoman is visited by the three Ulster champions by a remote lake, in which it is inferred that he actually lived. Cu Chulainn's single-combats take place at a ford, which, as Markale asserts, symbolised the junction between the two worlds.

In 'Branwen daughter of Llyr,' Mallolwch, King of Ireland, while out hunting, finds himself on the top of a mound overlooking a lake from whose waters step a red haired giant and his monstrous wife. In 'Owein,' the hero throws water from a fountain over a stone and a storm ensues. When it passes he finds himself in an unfamiliar, manifestly magical land.

The incident offers another example of the extraordinary durability of Celtic belief. Gerald of Wales mentions two wells with the capacity of inducing rain-storms. One, in Munster, when touched 'or even looked at,' deluged the entire province, ceasing only after a priest celebrated mass at a special chantry nearby and the well had been sprinkled with a mixture of holy water and 'the milk of a cow of one colour.' At the second, in Brittany, if water was accidentally spilt on a nearby rock, rain would fall 'even from a clear sky.'

The Celtic lands abound in folk-tales of underwater cities and palaces – possibly the origin of the Atlantis and other legends of submerged continents. Rhys records that in the late nineteenth century Welsh mothers still warned their children not to stray too far from their homes when the mist was thick lest they should be snatched away by the fairies to their dwellings beneath the lakes.

Also adopted from the Scythians was the Celtic practice of interring important warriors in their battle-waggons or chariots, together with their weapons and their favourite horses, slaughtered and stuffed, standing in the shafts. Examples have been excavated at Bell im Hunsruck, Bad Cannstadt near Stuttgart, and at La Gorge Meillet on the Marne. In the last case a second body was found at the site and is presumed to be that of the dead man's charioteer and personal attendant.

An oblique reference to the practice occurs in an episode in the Ulster Cycle in which Cu Chulainn, awakened from sleep by noise outside, goes to discover its cause. An image of nightmare greets him: an old man, supporting himself on a staff, walks by the side of a chariot. In it stands a hideous old hag and it is drawn by a horse with a single leg kept upright by the chariot-pole driven horizontally through its body and held in place by a peg where the end of the pole breaks through the frontal bone of the skull. The whole incident is vague, perhaps intentionally, perhaps because the copyist did not understand its significance, but the pole through the body secured by a peg at the forehead precisely evokes waggon-burial since this was the method used to keep the stuffed horse upright. The fact that the old man is carrying a hazel-wand helps to identify the couple as from the Other World.

Scythic and Celtic 'waggon burial' must have been intended to allow the sleeping warrior to awaken fully armed in his people's hour of crisis and is thus connected with the Celtic belief in the reawakening of heroes like Finn and Arthur.

The Scythians were the first people to use the horse as a draught-animal and passed their knowledge on to the Celts who, by the time they were known to the classical world, were so renowned for horsemanship and horse breeding that the Greek and Latin equine vocabularies – hence our own – consist almost exclusively of Celtic loan-words. In battle they were particularly feared for chariot-fighting and the pride taken in the skill is recorded in the myths. In 'The Intoxication of the Ulstermen' Loeg, Cu Chulainn's charioteer, is described as possessing the three skills of his craft: turning, backing, and leaping over chasms.

The veneration for the horse is confirmed archaeologically by its frequent representation. Besides coins, it is found on the Gundestrup Cauldron, as well as on widely distributed artefacts and on hill-figures such as the White Horse of Uffington, while horses' skulls have even been found in the underground grain silos in the Iron Age hill-fort at Danebury in Hampshire. It is further attested, not only by the existence in the Celtic pantheon of horse-gods like the Continental Epona, but also by the equine associations of many others. An alternative name of In Dagda is Eochaid Ollathair, by derivation meaning 'The Horse Father,' while the horse-elements 'Eoch-" and 'Ech-" repeatedly occur in the names of characters as in Etain Echrade, heroine of 'The Wooing of Etain,' said to be the most beautiful woman in all Ireland. The full name of Mark or

March, the king in 'Tristan and Isolt,' is 'March ap Meirchiawn,' 'Horse son of Horses.'[9]

March is a masculine cognate for the Irish Macha whose horse-nature is manifest in 'The Labour Pains of the Ulstermen,' where she is pitted against race-horses. In fact, after laying her curse on the men of the province, Macha vanishes from view, though one cannot help wondering whether she does not resume equine form for Cu Chulainn's horse is called 'Liath Macha,' which can mean both 'Grey of Macha' and 'Grey Macha.'

Horse characteristics are also discernible in Rhiannon. She is punished for her alleged killing of the infant Pryderi by being made to carry visitors to her husband's court on her back, and when rescued from the Castle of the Golden Bowl it is said that among the ordeals she was forced to endure was that of having to wear the 'collars worn by asses after they have been carrying hay.' Like Macha, she cannot be caught even by the fastest horse in Pwyll's stable.

An additional equine-link is that her child is recovered outside a stable just after the mare in it has foaled. This hints at a link with the very confused story of the birth of Cu Chulainn. That his mother, Dechtine, as well as being Conchobhar's daughter, is also his charioteer obviously gives her a horse association. But her seduction by Lugh takes place at a remote and mysterious house to which she and the rest of her party are led by bird song – an additional parallel with Rhiannon who, in 'Branwen Daughter of Llyr,' has a troupe of singing birds. While in the house, one of its women occupants goes into labour and bears a boy simultaneously with a mare dropping two foals. In the morning the company awaken to find the house has vanished, though Dechtine still has in her arms the newborn baby boy whom she adopts but who later dies. Through a vision she learns she is pregnant by Lugh, a matter of considerable embarrassment when her father betrothes her to Sualdam. She resolves her problem by 'lying down in the bed and crushing the child within her' and, in due course, Sualdam fathers Setanta, nicknamed Cu Chulainn, on her.

It is generally agreed that the original of this story has been badly mangled, particularly since it is plain from later passages that Lugh, in spite of Dechtine's self-induced abortion, still regards Cu Chulainn as his son. And it is surely strange that the woman in the disappearing house and the mare bear at the same time? The story has so many similarities to that of Pryderi's birth that one is led to speculate whether the two accounts are not superimposed on an earlier narrative in which both Irish and British heroes (or they are one and same?) are born of mares.

---

9 The fashion for equine-names seems to have extended itself to personal names: Cartimandua means 'The Little Pony.'

For much of the Celtic obsession with horses, Scythic mediation must have been responsible, but it may also have deeper roots to be found among the peoples from whom both Celts and Scythians sprang – the Indo-Europeans.

The term is a construct arising from the realisation in the seventeenth and eighteenth centuries that a number of languages showed not only grammatical and syntactical affinities, but had more words in common than could be accounted for by borrowings. This led to the postulation of a root-race with a single language from whom most of the peoples of Europe (the Hungarians, Finns and Turks are the principal exceptions), the Indians, and the Iranians, as well as the Scythians, Celts, Hittites, Greeks and Romans in the ancient world, have all evolved.

The theory of a common race has since been borne out by other evidence and, though its actual homeland is debated, opinion is gradually hardening on an area round the Volga basin. Here its members would have been conveniently placed to embark on their mass-migrations.

As words exist to describe concepts, vocabulary can be a guide to lifestyle For example, in all the Indo-European languages the words for numbers from one to a thousand are very similar and, as number-words are not found in all societies, they point to the existence among them of a comparatively sophisticated reckoning system, possibly decimal, before their dispersal in a series of separate waves around 2000 to 1500 bc.

Besides word correspondence, others are now recognised, particularly in mythology. An instance is the motif of magic apples. In Greek myth they grow in the Garden of Hesperides and, though their presence in the alien environment of the 'Sons of Tuirenn' may be the interpolation of a late storyteller, islands of apples occur in 'Maeldun' and, in the British Matter, Avalon takes its name from the Celtic word for apple. Apples are also found in Norse myth. Idun keeps the apples of perpetual youth which preserve the gods from the ravages of time, while Frey sends eleven apples to Gerda as a marriage proposal. This suggests the motif may go back to a shared Indo-European tradition.

In one of the *Tain* stories, Cu Chulainn inadvertently kills his own son. Son-slayings are also found in the Persian and German traditions.

Idris Foster draws attention to two other repeated motifs which are found in 'Kulhwch and Olwen.' One of the tasks assigned to the hero and his companions is to procure the flax for Olwen's wedding veil. They succeed with the aid of friendly ants. As the writer says, the entire incident, including the detail of the lame ant in 'Kulhwch,' is also found in a Slavonic version. The other is that of the oldest animals. In their quest for Mabon's prison, the companions, through Gwyrhyr Interpreter of Tongues, consult a succession of creatures, each older than the last. The whole incident is so closely paralleled in an Indian tale that, as Foster says, one must have been derived from the other.

Although the Scythians may have been the first to use the horse for draught purposes, it had been kept for its milk from long before and so would have been known to and probably bred by the original Indo-Europeans, which accounts for its occurrence in so many diverse milieux. Greek mythology has its horse-eared King Midas as counterpart for the Irish Labraidh Lorc and King March. The Scythians offered horses to their gods and Herodotus mentions the Persians as doing the same; there was also the Indian custom of *asamvedha*, in which one of the wives of a king ritually copulated with a sacrificed stallion.

If we are to believe Gerald of Wales, something similar, though involving a king and a mare, went on in Ireland in his own lifetime. With appropriate clerical repugnance, he describes a royal accession rite at Kenelcunil in northern Ulster at which the new king had public intercourse with a mare which was subsequently slaughtered and stewed. During the cooking, the king bathed and drank some of the broth, and the meat, when ready, was consumed by the assembly. As Markale makes clear, what we have in both the Indian and Irish instances is a symbolical marriage, and such ritual coupling with divine-mares could account for the birth of beings like Cu Chulainn and Pryderi, in whom human, godlike and, to some extent, equine qualities are conjoined. The fact that in Scythian, Persian, Indian and Celtic cases the sacrificial animals are white is further collateral proof of a link.

What is true of the horse, is also true of many of the other Celtic cult-creatures. Among those occurring in the myths are the salmon of knowledge, the stag, the boar or pig, the bull, the eagle, and the swan. Gwyrhyr Interpreter of Tongues in 'Kulhwch' is plainly a Druid since the ability to communicate with animals was a gift attributed to them. The creatures he consults include an owl, a stag, an eagle and, finally, an enormous Severn salmon, the oldest creature of all and the only one who knows where Mabon is held. Accompanied by Kai, Gwyrhyr is carried to his prison on its back. The scene recalls the Cernunnos panel on the Gundestrup Cauldron where one of the figures surrounding the central one of the horned god sits astride what is usually taken to be a dolphin but which might equally well be a large salmon.

The main subject of the story is the hunt of the magic boar Twrc Trwyth, which means that salmon, eagle, stag, and boar all figure in it. In the Irish Matter, Tuan tells his Christian auditors that during his successive lives he has been each of them and in 'Math' the magicians Gilvaethy and Gwydion are also transformed first into stags, then into boars, though in this case the final transformation is into a wolf. In the same story Lleu becomes an eagle.

The boar is shown on the crests of the helmets worn by the warriors on another of the Gundestrup panels and a torc-wearing stone figure from

Euffigneix in France has one incised on his chest. Both indicate an importance attached to the animal which is confirmed mythologically. The boar was primarily a quarry of the chase and the antiquity of the boar-hunt motif in stories like 'Kulhwch' and 'Manawydan,' as well as in medieval Arthurian legend, is proved by a Bronze Age votive waggon, about the size of a child's toy, found at Merida in Spain. On it a mounted and spear-wielding huntsman, with a dog at his feet, is chasing a boar.

We also have references to other members of the species as well as to their keepers. The two magicians of the *Tain* were first of all swineherds. Kulhwch was born in a pigsty (his name means 'Pig-run'). When Lleu, impaled by Goronwy's spear, flies off as an eagle, Gwydion sets out to track him down. He finds him perched in an oak tree beneath which a sow is feeding. Often there are underworld associations: the pigs which the magician Gwydion appropriates from Pryderi were said to have come originally from Annwvyn.

Another cult-animal, the bull, occurs in Celtic epigraphy and iconography as *Tarvos Trigaranos*, 'the bull with three cranes' found at Notre Dame and Treves, in the three horned bull representations found in Belgium, and the divine bull, *Deiotarus* (= Bull God), from Galatia. *Donnotaurus*, another bull known from epigraphy, may be the 'Brown Bull of Cuailnge' that became the *causus belli* between Ulster and Connaught.

Among Scythian items in the Hermitage Museum at Leningrad are a mask representing a stag equipped with a fine set of branching antlers, dated to the fifth century BC, as well as a gold stag about a foot in length dated to the sixth century and, though the stylistic resemblances between these and Celtic animal representations leave no doubt about the prototypes, once again the true origins of many of these cult-creatures may lie deeper.

Boars and pigs figure repeatedly in Greek mythology and, like the Celtic ones, usually have chthonic associations. They were rooting in the vicinity when Persephone, daughter of Demeter, was abducted by Hades. The name of the swineherd attending them, Eubouleus, had in earlier times been one of the cognomens of the Lord of the Underworld himself. In the *Odyssey* Circe, interpreted by some as Persephone's alter ego, entertains Odysseus at a palace with marked underworld qualities. While she tries to seduce him, his companions are turned into pigs. A pig was required sacrifice from initiates into the Eleusinian Mysteries connected with Demeter, Persephone's mother.

Among Indo-European mythologies in which the bull figures is the Hindu, where it is linked with Indra, Varuna, and Mitra. There is the bull of Minos in Crete, and in one of his many seductions of mortal women Zeus takes on the bull-form to couple with Europa. In the seduction of Leda Zeus becomes a swan, another creature important to the Celts. In 'The Boyhood Deeds of Cu Chulainn' the hero, out for the first time in the chariot given him by King Conchobhar, causes a flock of swans, apparently hypnotised, to fly back to the palace with him. In 'The Wooing of Etain' both the heroine and Mider are transformed into swans and Caer, the dream-girl in 'Oengus,' alternates between human and swan forms. When Oengus first sees her in her avian manifestation, with her 'thrice fifty' companions about her, all but Caer are paired together with silver chains. This helps to confirm the very early age of the story, for Bronze Age swan-heads with rings and links of chain have been found at Celtic sites in central Europe.

Professor Ross stresses the differences between the Celtic swan stories and those of the continental tradition, as in the German *Lohengrin* and the Russian fairy-tale which formed the plot for Tchaikovski's ballet *Swan Lake;* but it is difficult not to believe they are part of a common heritage.

Other birds common to almost all Indo-European cultures are the eagle and the raven. In Greece the eagle is associated with Zeus; in the Persian *Avesta* it nests in the Tree of All-Healing; in the Hindu *Rig Veda* it is an eagle that brings humans the gift of the ritual drug *soma,* enabling them to make contact with the divine. The story is probably linked with the Norse legend of Odin, who turns himself into an eagle to retrieve the sacred mead stolen by the giant Suttung. Lugh, too, is associated with the eagle, whose form his spirit takes in the story of Blodeuwydd's infidelity.

Linked with both Odin and Apollo, especially in his Hyperborean manifestation, is the raven and it is perhaps only logical that the Celtic raven should invariably be associated with war and slaughter since it is a bird of carrion. Even in late times soldiers on the march, spotting them perching, would take it as a presage of coming battle.

The Irish Morrigan and her cronies can turn themselves into a flock of ravens and Bran is linked with the bird by name As the Morrigan is a goddess who haunts the battle-field, so Bran also often plays the role of war god. Dillon in *The Celtic Realms* quotes a paean describing him as 'protector of hosts,' 'fierce raider,' 'harsh spear,' 'sun of warriors,' 'bloody wolf,' and 'dog of the pack.' It was no doubt because of this that the Celtic attackers of Rome and Delphi, when asked who was their leader, replied 'Brennus,' a latinisation of 'Bran.'

Bran and the Morrigan may at some early stage have been united, perhaps as husband and wife, for in the story of Bran's Miraculous Head, which survives eighty years after severance from his body, the companions are entertained by the singing of the Birds of Rhiannon, who has been convincingly equated with the Morrigan.[10] His is not, of course, the only Miraculous Head, for there is also that of Sualdam.

---

10 *White Hill,* where Bran's head was buried, is said to be the present site of the Tower of London and an ancient tradition links him with the ravens there.

The motif may well be another of Indo-European provenance. In Norse myth the head of the wise giant Mimir, decapitated by the Vanir, guards one of the wells under the World Tree where it is visited by gods seeking its counsel, and Odin was said to have exchanged an eye for a draught from the well. In Greece, after the prophet Orpheus has been torn to pieces by the frenzied Maenads, his head floats ashore at Lesbos, where it continues prophesying until rebuked by Apollo who arrogates the privilege to himself alone.

Reference in the last section to Lugh, Mercury, Odin, and Apollo raises the question of Indo-European gods. Georges Dumezil has attempted to show that three types – representing the magical, knightly and agricultural aspects of life – are found in all their pantheons. Though not all accept his argument in toto, there are grounds for accepting the idea of Indo-European gods. The Greek Uranus is plainly cognate with the Hindu Varuna; Mitra, with the Persian Mithras; and an Indo-European root 'Deiwo' is the source of god-words like 'Deo,' 'Dieu,' 'Theos' and even 'Deva' and 'Devil.'

In any case, the fact that Caesar could confidently attach the name 'Mercury' to the god usually taken to be Lugh can only mean that he saw an equivalence with the Roman deity, who is himself equated with the Greek Hermes. Hermes, Mercury, and Lugh are all guardians of the highway and the patrons of travellers and commerce, as is the Norse Odin who is linked to Lugh through the common attribute of the eagle

I am again indebted to Tolstoy for pointing out another connection which occurs in the account of Lugh's death. He is, of course, struck by the spear of Goronwy, and Odin, hanging nine days and nights from the World Tree, a 'sacrifice of myself to myself' as the Havamal poem expresses it, is also wounded with a spear.

Another shared characteristic of Lugh and Odin is their patronage of art and poetry. On the other hand, for the Greeks and Romans this was primarily the function of Apollo, whose Celtic equivalent is normally taken to be Belinus. Odin, Apollo, and Belinus are all solar deities. So is Lugh. In one story, the Fomorian tyrant Bress, dazzled by a light from the west in the morning sky, asks his Druids if the sun has risen from that quarter this particular morning. He is told that it is 'the radiance of the face of Lugh.'

However, Lugh and Apollo are both gods of healing and the former shares one other characteristic with the latter and with Odin – remorselessness. Odin manifests it when he demands that his favourite Starkad should offer himself as blood-sacrifice in repayment for past favours; Lugh in his refusal to save the Sons of Tuirenn, despite the pleas of their father and the fact they have fulfilled all the terms of the fine imposed on them.

Though similarities of belief can be found between the Celts and most of the Indo-European peoples, there is one culture where these are to be found in the greatest number.

Detailed comparisons with Hindu material (for instance, bardic metres resemble not only those used in Greece, but also those in the *Rig Veda*, the earliest known Indo-European verse) has prompted studies of Druidism and Hindu Brahminism that have revealed numerous correspondences, just as, according to Caesar, the Druids and the knights were the two most privileged classes in Celtic society, so were the Brahmins and Kshatriyas in India, while Hinduism shares with Druidism a belief in reincarnation. The cross-legged pose associated with the Buddha is repeated on many Celtic artefacts, including the Gundestrup Cauldron.

The Brahmins – who according to Max Weber's definition were, like the Druids, a caste of royal magicians, prophets and counsellors – were the custodians of doctrine and the law-givers. They held their law to be of divine origin, and the fact that many of the tracts are in verse makes it certain, in Weber's view, that they and, probably all other Brahminic teaching, was at one time, like the Druidic, part of an oral tradition.

D. A. Binchy and the late Professor Myles Dillon, both of whom studied Druidism and Hinduism exhaustively, draw attention to many other parallels. Just as the Celts recognised ten forms of marriage so Brahminism had eight, many the same. The system of suretyship and the use of fasting to enforce claims or redress for grievances are also found in India. No less striking is the system of the 'appointed daughter' (*putrika,* in India) – that is to say, a daughter appointed by a man who had no sons to share all the privileges normally reserved to a male heir.

So many far-reaching similarities presuppose a common source, but since the geographical separation between the Indian subcontinent and Celtic Europe makes direct transmission in either direction inconceivable it can only have come from one to which both had had access before the parting of the ways.

But what was the nature of that source?

Chapter 9

SHAMANISM AND THE MYTHS

Reading the descriptions of the Druids in the classical texts one cannot help being struck by a surprising omission: nowhere are they spoken of as a priesthood. Yet, on the face of it, the word would surely have been the simplest way of explaining them to their readers? These contemporary observers must therefore have had a reason for avoiding the term, the most likely being that, to them, the Druids appeared so different from the priests with whom they were familiar that the word was inappropriate. The Druids were a phenomenon, and Caesar can have devoted so much space to Gaulish religion and its ministers only because he regarded it in this light.

In point of fact, the nearest we ever get to a generic term is in the *Natural History* where Pliny the Elder calls them 'magicians,' a word deriving from the Magi of the Persians. The author was aware of its etymology for he adds that the Druids behaved as if magic had been invented in Britain rather than Persia.

But if to Pliny's eyes there were similarities between Persians and Druids, there were others – as we have seen – between them and the Brahmins of India. The Magi, Brahmins, and Druids were indeed bracketed together as men of surpassing wisdom by two eminent figures of the Ancient World. But, apart from the fact that all three share a common, Indo-European birthplace, is there anything else that unites them?

The immutable sequence of night and day and of the seasons, the phenomena of nature – storm, earthquake, volcano, birth and, particularly, death – must always have been infinitely mysterious to the human mind, but it was probably during the hunting stage that the need to placate what were seen as supernatural forces first arose.

It is likely that the inflicting of death entailed by the quest for food caused such stress that the hunters were driven to finding ways of alleviating it by seeking to pacify the spirits of those whom their activities had ejected violently from their bodies. Initially these took – and in some cases, still take – the form of communal post-hunt rituals. For example, the bones of a slaughtered animal would be taken back to a place known to be frequented by the herd and there re-assembled so that its now homeless spirit might find and reoccupy them. Others were more elaborate and might, for example, involve drawing a picture of the quarry on the ground before the hunt and afterwards attaching to it some of the animal's skin. As representations always carry some of the qualities of the reality, the combination of this with parts of the actual creature was seen as a re-creation.

Such placatory gestures suffered from an inherent disadvantage: there was no way of judging their acceptability to the slaughtered creature. It was to resolve the problem that a specially-endowed being, the shaman, evolved. He can be broadly defined as one who, as the result of a personal crisis, often self-induced, but which included his own symbolic death and resurrection, acquired an extraordinary rapport with and mastery over the environment in its natural and especially its supernatural aspects. In particular, he acquires the gift of inducing trances in which he can leave his mortal body. It is this last capacity that defines him, though as a kind of bonus – signalling his special relationship with the supernatural – the shaman also gains the gifts of prophecy, clairvoyance, and clairaudience.

Through his trance, the 'spirit-flight,' he can visit the spirit realm and negotiate on behalf of his fellows with its largely animal inhabitants. To make himself recognizable, he dresses himself in a costume representing the species he wants to contact – a cloak of the animal's skin, antlers if it is a horned creature or, in the case of birds, feathers or a beaked-mask.

Often the induction of trance will be assisted by taking what we know as hallucinatory drugs, but which, to the shaman, were powerful magical substances. Besides cannabis, the fruit of the peyote cactus, the red-capped mushroom and extracts from the poppy and the east Mediterranean pine, *Ephedra fragilis,* most of the so-called 'hard drugs' have served him at one time or other.

After repeated Other World visits, he will achieve an intimacy with one of those who dwell there. Friendship will be reciprocated by benefactions to his tribe, who, in turn, will adopt the creature as its totem, venerating representations of it and refraining from killing its species.

In this way the whole of tribal life becomes inseparably bound up with its relations with the totem. It goes to war in defence of its honour; it adopts those rules and customs which the shaman, its mouthpiece, recommends as pleasing to it. Usually a tribe will trace its ancestry back to its totem-animal, so that it becomes a communal ancestor.

In this way, as an extension of his role as mediator between his people and its totem, the shaman also becomes its historian, guardian of its myths, epic-singer, keeper of lineages and law-giver. Furthermore, all misfortunes, collective or individual, being an expression of the totem's displeasure, the malignity of enemy totems, or even the activity of evil shamans (or, worse, of witches!), the shaman is called upon to use his influence with the spirits to secure their removal. He is, therefore, the healer, which Eliade regards as one of his most essential gifts.

But with his unique personal knowledge of the Other World, when any member of the community dies it is for him to guide his or her spirit to its new resting place. That is say, he is communal psychopomp or conductor of souls.

The antiquity of the shaman is proved by his representation in cave-drawings going back 20 to 30 thousand years, such as the famous 'Sorcerer of Les *Trois Freres,* in southern France. He is also of worldwide occurrence, which is to say he is invariably to be found practising in societies with hunting and fishing or pastoral-nomadic economies, though by the time the second stage is reached the totem will probably have evolved into gods in human form.

Exactly how the transition took place is not known for certain, and there is undoubtedly more than one way. In many cases it would be by a simple evolutionary progression from theriomorphic, or animal-deities, into anthropomorphic, or human ones, often with some of the animal characteristics being retained after the change. The process can be seen at work in the Hindu gods and in those of Egypt with their human bodies and animal heads, and even in those cultures where the physical metamorphosis has apparently been completed relics of the totemic past survive, not only in the animal qualities of the deities or their attributes, such as the owl of Athena or the bull of Mithras, but in the ideology of the shaman himself. Michael Harrier devotes a chapter of his book *The Way of the Shaman,* in effect a do-it-yourself manual, to 'power animals,' creatures which can be said to 'inhabit' the shaman and act as his guardian spirits. Though they are relics of a totemic past, 'power animals' are to be found in contexts far removed from it.

Another way in which the shift to anthropomorphic gods took place involves the shaman more directly. In the way of all flesh, passing permanently over to the Other World, he there becomes available to his living successors, a totem in human form, or what we would recognise as a god. One of the stages in the process is exemplified in the practice of the South American Guarani Indians who preserve the bones of their dead medicinemen in special huts where they go to consult them and make offerings.

The divine shaman is to be found in almost all pantheons and retains most of the characteristics of his mortal counterparts. He continues to act as intermediary between the two worlds. Like the mortal shaman he is a psychopomp. He is the animator of prophets. Having been his people's mythologue in life, he is now the inspirer of poets and artists. He is the divine healer. Most of all he is the magician, the god of magic in Dumezil's trio.

But he also retains mastery of the natural world and its inhabitants, indeed both his powers and his domain are now extended. He is truly the 'Lord of the Animals.'

Among the last surviving pastoral-nomads of Europe – the Lapps – shamans (*noaidit*) were still operating in the eighteenth century. Though numbers decline by the year, cultures in which shamanism survives are still to be found. Thanks to the field studies of men like Knud Rasmussen and Sergei Shirogokorov, and to the great cross-cultural surveys like the now world-renowned ones by Mircea Eliade and Vilmos Dioszegi, we now have a full and clear idea of the forms and structures of shamanism.

We know that in order to become a shaman, the novice, having undergone his initiatory crisis, completes his training at the feet of an elder of the calling, that this can be of extremely long duration, and that all instruction is oral.

We know that the shaman's function as mediator with the spirit world is, as might be expected, one which gives him immense power and prestige. Frequently, possibly in conclave with other tribal shamans, he will be responsible for the appointment of a new chieftain; occasionally, as in certain instances in Siberia, the home of shamanism, he may himself accede to the chieftainship.

When not on his soul-journeys, he is usually to be found living in the wilderness, in places far from the habitations of men, 'close to nature' as we might say. And it is thence that those wishing to consult him must make their way and that he will hold his seances, public or private.

In a relic of his totemistic past, his closest companions are the creatures of the wild with whom, like Gwyrhyr Interpreter of Tongues in 'Kulhwch,' he is believed to be able to communicate. Novice medicine-men in North and South America must learn to imitate the voices of animals: during seances, Siberian and Eskimo shamans emit the cries of birds and wild animals. Often a particular animal or bird, a tame fox or a raven, will serve him as a kind of familiar and, in spirit-form, may accompany him or appear to him in his trance.

However, the shaman does not merely imitate birds or animals; he is credited with the ability to transform himself into them. Chukchee and Eskimo shamans can turn themselves into wolves; the Lapp *noaidit* could become wolves, bears, reindeer, fish; Semang shamans, tigers.

The fact that during his trance the shaman's soul, as it were, takes flight means that it is itself often likened to a bird, expecially the high-soaring eagle. One Siberian people, the Yakut, even regard the eagle as a proto-shaman and, as an aid to flight, almost all the North American medicine-men include its feathers in their costume.

In some cultures the shaman, once initiated, is believed to undergo a change of sex at the behest of the spirits and will take to wearing female clothing, even speaking with a high-pitched voice. Tribes among whom this occurs include the Damchadal, the Asiatic Eskimo, the Koryak, and, outside this region, among some of those of Indonesia and the Americas. As we know, it was their supposed sex-change which has led some authorities to suggest that the Scythian Enarees may have been eunuchs. It is not necessarily the case. Though both self-emasculation and homosexuality is known,

Eliade discusses the Chukchee shamans who may, in some instances, marry other men, though more often continue to live with their wives and father children.

To attribute to shamanism a coherent body of moral or ethical doctrine would be totally to misunderstand its nature. Morality involves generalisations applicable to all sorts and conditions of men, and such is not the shaman's province. His concern is with the specific instance and he is consulted as one consults a doctor or fortune teller. He is what Pliny calls the Druids – a magician – and as Emil Durkheim says, the magician has a clientele, where the priest has a congregation.

Nevertheless, wherever shamanism occurs, whether in Siberia, the Arctic, the Americas or the Australian outback, similar symbols, metaphors, and concepts occur.

Thus, our own and the Other World are regarded as coexistent though the supernatural forces are concentrated at a Great Centre, which can take the form of a sacred mountain, as among the Altaic Tartars, or a tree, as among certain Ostyak tribes. The centre links the three worlds. The roots which support the great trunk of the Norse Yggdrasil pass into the realms of the Aesir, the frost giants and the dead. Its branches, stretching up to the heavens, overshadow the whole earth. And it is here that the gods abide, holding their assemblies round its trunk.

Wherever a tree is involved it may be any one of many kinds, but it is not unusual for it to be a nut- or fruit-bearing one, its crop itself possessing magical qualities. In any case, whether the centre is represented by tree, mountain, or in any other way, it is often associated with a water source – a river, lake, or well.

The shaman's soul-journey to reach it involves negotiating a tumultuous river, the frontier between the two worlds, usually by means of a narrow and perilous bridge.

In the Other World all things are the mirror-image of our own. Right becomes left. It is day there when it is night on earth, for which reason most shamanistic seances take place in the hours of darkness.

It is possible to trace the ideology of shamanism behind many beliefs. Since he came into existence to resolve the problems caused by the hunter's unhousing of spirits, one can see how those wandering spirits could be thought capable of taking up their abode in other bodies or in the womb. In this way reincarnation can be traced back to its influence. So can the concept of cosmic balance, of the total interdependence of every single element in the universe, for it was to maintain this balance and restore it after the disturbance caused by the activities of the hunters that the shaman came into existence. Even from so brief and simplified a description it is obvious that the shamanistic thread runs through the mythologies of all the Indo-European peoples.

Among other Hindu gods who play the part, Shiva-Prasupati is recognizable as a 'Lord of the Animals.' Apollo is portrayed in the same guise and shares with Odin patronage of healing, prophecy, magic, and the inspiration of art. The latter plays the role of psychopomp, conducting the spirits of slain heroes to Valhalla. Hermes, whose helmet is adorned with the shamanic eagle's wings, fulfils a similar function in Greek myth. In Greek mythology the eagle itself is also associated with Zeus, in the Norse myths with Odin, who is also attended by two ravens, Hugin and Munin, representing thought and memory; the same bird is one of the attributes of Apollo.

In Hinduism the Great Centre is Mount Meru (or Sumeru), the home of Seven Sages, themselves reminiscent of shamans. In Greece there are two centres: Mount Olympus where Zeus reigns as king, and Mount Parnassus where Apollo has his oracular shrine at Delphi, the *omphalos* or navel of the world. The tree as Great Centre occurs in Norse mythology as Yggdrasil, beneath which was the wonder-working well of Mimir.

The Brahminic ritual drug soma, named after the moon-goddess of Hinduism, is plainly the descendant of those used by the shamans to assist in inducing the trance

What are equally unmistakable are the shamanistic elements in Druidism. From the classical references we know the Druids to have been prophets, healers, magicians, and custodians of law; that their apprenticeship entailed long and intensive studies in which all teaching was oral, and that having qualified, like the shaman, 'they had their abode in the depths of forests,' but, like him too, still managed to play a central, even supreme role in their society.

The animal representations found by archaeology correspond with the totemic animals of shamanism, and especially those associated with Indo-European shamanism.

The typical shamanistic image of the Other World as a place where everything is the reverse of our own would explain why Caesar mentions the Druidic festivals as being celebrated at night.

In Cernunnos, as represented on the Gundestrup Cauldron and in other contexts, we have a typical 'Lord of the Animals' who is even shown wearing a span of antlers, the kind of headdress a shaman might adopt to make himself recognizable to the creatures of the Other World.

Just as shamanism has its 'Great Centre,' so we are told by Caesar that the annual Druidic convention took place in what was regarded as the centre of Gaul in 'a consecrated place.' What is more, the word 'centre' recurs among Celtic placenames. Milan, in northern Italy, the Romans' Cisalpine Gaul, comes from 'Mediolanum.' In Ireland, there is Meath, a name which means 'the Centre.'

The tree as centre is suggested by the Celtic word bile, used to designate a sacred tree and occurring in place-names as separate as Bilum in

Denmark and Bilem in France. It is also significant that, though the ash and the yew are among trees found in the myths, most common is the oak and that one interpretation of the word 'Druid' is 'the wise man of the oak.'

When we turn to the myths the shamanic echoes become deafening. A typical case is 'Math son of Mathonwy'. Although all the characters are presented in human guises, their animal nature is only thinly covered. Math, for instance, actually means 'bear'. Blodeuedd, Lleu's wife, is an owl. Arianrhod means, literally, 'Silver Wheel', possibly a metaphor for a spider's web, and some scholars have conjectured that she might be a Celtic analogue of the Greek Ariadne whose name also links her with the spider.

Taking the Matters of Ireland and Britain as a whole, we find residues of totemic mares and horses, traced to Scythia and Indo-European mediation, exhibited by Rhiannon and Macha, in heroes like Pryderi and Cu Chulainn, or in the ears of the Irish Labraidh Lorc and the British March, 'horse son of horses'.

Kulhwch is linked with the pig both by his name, 'Pig-run', and his place of birth. The fact that pork-eating is prohibited in many religions suggests that it was once a totem whose flesh it was always forbidden to eat, and something of its sacred character seems to have survived into Christian times, for in the early Middle Ages it was used to indicate where religious establishments were to be erected.

Similar totemistic prohibitions may explain Cu Chulainn's geis against eating dog-flesh or Conaire's against eating bird. Conaire is supposed to have been the son of a bird and it was usual, especially for chieftains, to claim the totemic animal as parent.

Another Indo-European totemic creature, the eagle, is of course the form assumed by Lleu after he is speared by Goronwy and, as it stands as a symbol of the shaman's spirit-flight, one can only agree with Tolstoy that the god's transformation signals his magical character, even if it were not explicitly stated in *The Book of Taliessin*.

Among other birds, the raven occurs several times. But there are, besides, the Birds of Rhiannon who entertain Bran's friends and they may possibly be the ones in 'Owein' whose singing is the sweetest the hero has ever heard. Another character in 'Owein', the one-eyed black giant, is almost certainly the horned-god Cernunnos, already identified as a Celtic epiphany of 'Lord of the Animals'. He is described as 'keeper of the forest' and demonstrates his lordship by striking a stag with his cudgel. The roar of pain it emits serves to summon all the other animals until, so the teller of the story says, there was hardly room for him to stand. At an order from the giant, they bow their heads and worship as 'obedient men do their lord'.

Owein's black giant exhibits the Druidic – and shamanistic – predilection for wild and remote places which has already enabled us to identify the Arthurian 'hermits,' such as the two encountered by Peredur. In the Irish Matter we have an instance in 'Bricriu's Feast,' where the three Ulster champions, wishing to consult the powerful Druid Uath mac Imoman, seek him out at his home by (or, possibly, in) a distant lake.

Uath affords an instance of another skill possessed by Druid and shaman: that of shape-shifting. Uath's many gifts include the ability to 'change himself into any form he wished.' It seems to have been one he shared with the magician pig-keepers of the *Tain Bo Cuailnge* who go through a series of transformations before being reborn as bulls, while the harpers of Cain Bile turn themselves into deer to evade the pursuers who take them for enemy spies. During the hunt for the boar, Twrc Trwyth, Kulhwch is told: 'He was once a king, but was turned into a boar by God on account of his sins.'

We repeatedly find Druids in the shamanic role of prophets. When a scream so penetrating that the men of the household seize their weapons issues from the belly of Fedlimid's pregnant wife, Cathbad predicts that her child will be 'a tall, lovely, long-haired woman,' but that she will be a source of contention and slaughter – as proves to be the case.

They are also healers. In 'The Wasting Sickness of Cu Chulainn,' his wife, Emer, bitterly laments the failure of the Ulstermen to seek a cure for his condition and angrily compares this behaviour with her husband's for, she says, if any of his friends had fallen sick he would scour the land for a Druid to cure him.

Cu Chulainn's patron, King Conchobhar, has his household physician Finghin who, in one story, is summoned to the bedside of the seriously wounded Cethern and, because of his superior skill, is able to cure him after others have failed. Finghin is less successful in treating the king who has a slingshot ball lodged in his forehead after a brawl. He decides it is too risky to operate and though Conchabhar survives for seven years with the embedded missile, he meets his end when it bursts out as he is seized by ungovernable rage on hearing of Christ's crucifixion.

Though there is a Celtic god of healing in the Tuathan Diancecht, Lugh, like Odin and Apollo, seems also to have had a healing aspect. He snatches his son Cu Chulainn from the battlefield to cure him of his wounds and, in 'The Sons of Tuirenn,' his father is said to be Cian, himself the son of Diancecht and a greater physician than his father who was able only to provide Nuada with a false hand of silver, while Cian replaces the lost one, enabling him to return to the throne.

Lugh, also like Odin and Apollo, is the inspirer of poets, constantly invoked by the *filid* and frequently praised or shown in the most favourable light. Even his eagle-attribute seems to link him with poetry – a linkage also found in the shamanism of other cultures. Tuan's penultimate animal incarnation is as a sea-eagle.

If other traces of the shamanistic past have survived in the myths, so too have its fundamental beliefs. As we know, the Druids propagated the doctrine of reincarnation and we have already discussed examples of it. The theme of cosmic balance is given graphic mythological representation in 'Peredur.' Riding through a valley, he comes upon two meadows divided by a river. Black sheep graze in one, white sheep in the other. Whenever one of the white sheep bleats a black sheep crosses the river and joins the white flock, turning white itself in the process. When one of the black sheep bleats, the opposite occurs. With slight modification the same incident is found in the Irish 'The Voyages of Maeldun' where an island of black and white sheep is among the ports of call. The 'Maeldun' and the 'Peredur' stories both imply that the number of sheep in each case remain equal. The two colours symbolise the two worlds, and the transformation of white into black and vice versa the exchanges between mortal and Other Worlds. This brings to mind Caesar's statement that when a man was sick a surrogate-sacrifice would be offered.

Two additional details suggest that the 'Peredur' version may be older than the 'Maeldun' one. On one bank of the river, the hero sees a tall tree, half of it 'aflame from roots to crown,' while the other is decked in fresh green leaves. Surveying the scene from a nearby mound is 'a young lord' with two greyhounds who hospitably invites Peredur to his castle. When the offer is declined, he directs Peredur as to which of three roads he should take to continue his journey. Forked Other World road-junctions are themselves shamanistic and it is because of the dilemma they present to the uninitiated traveller that at death he needs the shaman's services as psychopomp.

Another shamanistic theme, the Great Centre, appears in the British 'Llud and Llevelys.' King Lludd, the Irish Nuada, plagued by oppressions, seeks the advice of Llevelys. He is instructed to measure out the length and breadth of his country, thereby discovering its exact centre. He does so, and at this point discovers, as Llevelys forecast, a dragons' lair. It is by overcoming the dragons' power that the oppressions are brought to an end.[11] In one of the tales of the Irish Diarmait, he visits what is plainly an Other World location. In the midst of a landscape of breathtaking loveliness stands a tree so huge that it overtops all the others. Delicious ripe fruit hang in clusters from it and nearby is a pool of crystal clear water. The fountain which gives Owein access to the Other World when he throws water from it over a stone also stands beneath 'a great tree with branches greener than the greenest fir.' Even more recurrent is the third of the shamanic motifs: the Narrow Bridge. To reach the island on which the Amazon Scatchach dwells, Cu Chulainn has to cross a bridge designed in such a way that the moment anyone tries to step on one end the far one rises

---

11   A dragon occurs at another centre, of course, namely Apollo's at Delphi and it is only by its slaughter that the young god is able to make the shrine his own.

in the air. Thrice he makes the attempt, but each time it defies him. It is only when his warrior-fury comes upon him that he is able to perform the Hero's Salmon Leap and get over successfully.

Elsewhere in the Irish Matter the bridge recurs as the Island of the Glass Bridge in 'The Voyages of Maeldun.' When Maeldun and his companions try to cross it to reach the brazen door to the castle at its far end, it throws them backward, like Scathach's. After several attempts they reach the door, but when they strike upon it, instead of opening it emits a melody so sweet they fall asleep. This is thrice repeated, but at their fourth attempt a beautiful woman in white opens the door and welcomes them.

Tolstoy points out a narrow bridge of iron and steel no more than half a foot wide which, in one of the traditional stories, the magician Merlin has to negotiate. Only those whose life is without blame can pass over it safely, a characteristic of the perilous bridges of many religions, including Islam and Persian Zoroastrianism.

One of the most famous bridges is the one Lancelot has to cross in his pursuit of the abducted Guinevere. It is no wider than the edge of a sword-blade – evoking the razor's edge of Buddhism – and, typically, a tumultuous stream flows beneath it.

Finally there is the essential capacity of the shaman: his ability to put himself into a state of trance in which he is believed to leave his own body. In the mythology it has to be said that there is a dearth of explicit examples, though the numerous stories of underwater cities that are so common in Celtic folk-lore may owe something to it. We know from the descriptions of those who, like Michael Harner, have experienced the trance at first-hand that in certain cases shamans can believe themselves plunging deep into waters until they arrive in a strange fantastical land. As we have seen, that water was a means of access to the Other World was a strongly held belief among the Celts.

There is, however, one unmistakable instance of shamanic trance. Consulted by King Ailill and Queen Mebd concerning a crisis in Connaught's fortunes, the Druid mac Roth dons a costume which, with its bull hide cloak and bird headdress, is identical with that worn by the classical shaman. So attired, he is described as 'rising up with the fire into the air and skies.' Here we have an almost verbatim description of a Siberian seance during which the performer will invariably be thought to leave on his spirit-flight by way of the smoke hole.[12]

---

12 Evidence as to whether the Druids used ritual drugs to aid trance is wholly circumstantial, coming partly from Pliny's description of the mistletoe-gathering ceremony, though the mistletoe-berry is not a hallucinogen, and partly from a folk-tradition that they extracted an opium-like substance from the poppy. It is also possible that the so-called 'magic mushroom' was used for Druidic ritual purposes.

For the general scarcity of recognizable descriptions there is, in my view, a simple explanation of which references to the Narrow Bridge provide a clue: much of the body of the myths actually consists of accounts of Other World visits, elements of which, such as those in 'Peredur,' 'Owein,' 'Manawydan,' and 'Gereint,' have already been touched on.

There is a consensus among scholars that Pwyll's meeting with Arawn is a visit to the underworld. Cu Chulainn's visit to the realm of Scathach is another and it is hard to believe that the strange islands visited by Maeldun and his friends belong to the quotidian world. By the same token, Lancelot's crossing of the Sword Bridge can be properly understood only if we recognise his journey's true destination, to which, in Chrétien de Troyes's version, we are offered several clues. It is while he is riding towards the bridge that he has the strange encounter with the Maid of the Mule and Chrétien tells us that, on the journey, he was in a state in which he had ceased to know 'whether he was alive or dead' and even forgot his own name.

At the bridge, instead of taking advantage of the protection of his armour against its sharp edges, he deliberately strips himself of it, so that he arrives on the far side cut and bleeding – an echo of the mutilations which shamans often inflict on themselves. Once he has made the crossing, he sees that the two fearsome lions he thought were guarding the far bank do not exist and that there is 'not a living creature there.' This, too, is typical of shamanism.[13]

A comparative study of shamanism and Celtic mythology would need a book in itself and these pages can claim to have examined only a few of the landmarks. They have, I hope, been sufficient to show that all the main characteristics of shamanism are present in the myths. The only way they could have entered is through Druidism. Hence, Celtic mythology is the 'topography of a supernatural reality,' a topography, furthermore, with roots certainly going back 3000 years, and probably a great deal further.

---

13 It is interesting in this connection that Hermann Lommel in *The World* of the *Early Hunters* suggests that Homer's *Odyssey* may be an account of a shamanic Other World visit. The thesis has much to commend it.

Chapter 10

WHAT THE MYTHS TELL US

So far we have seen how information gathered from other sources is reflected in the myths. For example, we know that in Ireland, when the king died, the royal Druids assembled, sacrificed an ox, made a broth of its flesh, then slept on its skin. In the dream that followed, the identity of the future king would be revealed. A reference to the *Tarbfeis* or bull-feast is found in the legend of Conaire and it may be the key to the significance of the ox-skin on which Rhonabwy's dream comes to him.

The 'adultery' motif, either inadvertent, as in the case of Tristan's with Isolt, or culpable, as in that of Lancelot's with Guinevere, must spring from the ritual marriage of king and territorial goddess of which we have evidence from a number of sources.

Probably linked with it are two others: that of the Blemished King and the rivalry between an older and a younger man for the affections of a young woman. The most obvious example is Kulhwch's attempt to prise Olwen from the grasp of her giant father Ysbaddaden, but it is also to be found in Tristan's rivalry with Mark for Isolt and that of Cu Chulainn with Forgall, Emer's father, for his daughter.

To be acceptable to his divine consort, the mortal king must be without physical imperfection. Both Nuada and Bress have to relinquish thrones when the one loses a hand in battle and the other develops skin-blotches. But this was not the only reason for the withdrawal of favour. It could come about because the king began to sink into the infirmities of age for, as we know from the *Tain*, Celtic deities, male or female, were possessed of gargantuan sexual appetites. Mebd, Queen-goddess of Connaught, tells her husband Ailill: 'I never had one man without another waiting in his shadow.' Elsewhere she is said to need thirty men a day, and only those who were her equal in stamina could remain her lovers.

Thus, as the goddess's husband aged so did she, while in sympathy with her womb the land itself became barren, the streams and lakes dry, and, even the birds fell silent, a situation reflected in the episode of the Fisher-King. Youth and fecundity are to be regained only by supplying her with a new lover, even if this necessitates the disposal of the old. Like Ysbaddaden in 'Kulhwch,' he is condemned to die when his daughter finds a mate. This feature of the story may be the key to its inner meaning: in high pagan times it was customary for the Celts to kill the reigning king and replace him by a younger one whenever the portents seem to indicate that this was what his divine spouse desired.

Ritual regicide also seems to lie at the heart of 'The Destruction of Da Derga's Hostel,' for just after King Conaire's arrival at the hostel the giantess demands entrance, reeling off her names, which include Samain (the time at which the events are said to be taking place) and Badb (literally, scald-crow). The Badb, presager of slaughter, is one of the forms the Morrigan could assume so that her appearance at this moment is an omen of disaster. Besides, Conaire is under *geis* never to admit a single woman after sunset. He is forced to do so when she impugns his hospitality and she remains as a witness to the whole bloody proceedings that follow, making her final appearance as Conaire lies dying.

What may be another allusion is contained in a story quoted by Powell. At Samain men from all over Ireland converge on Cruachain, the royal centre of Connaught, to woo a maiden. For each suitor, one of his people was secretly slain. The maiden must be the territorial goddesses whose goodwill is secured by these sacrifices and it is in this sense we must understand Queen Mebd's thirty lovers: they were sacrificial victims.

Often we depend on the myths to put information derived from other sources into context.

Archaeology may uncover magnificent native artefacts like the Gundestrup Cauldron, but their significance is clear only from references to mythological cauldrons with their ability to provide inexhaustible quantities of food or restore the dead to life

The frequent boar representations may tell us that the animal was of particular importance, but to understand its exact nature we have to turn to the descriptions of hunts such as those in 'Manawydan' and 'Kulhwch,' in both of which a supernatural boar is the quarry.

Similarly, the incidence of fish-forms is explained by the Salmon of Wisdom in the Matters of both Ireland and Britain. Its wisdom has often been gained by eating the hazelnuts falling from the magic tree overhanging the river, stream or well it inhabits; hazelnuts and hazel leaves have been recovered from a well at Ashill in Norfolk, while the Celtic word for hazel, *coll*, occurs in placenames and in the names of the several mythical characters.

Myths, then, can help with the interpretation of material from other sources; but can they shed any light on Druidism? Though, in view of the debased state in which we have received the myths, caution is necessary, there are motifs so recurrent in both the Irish and British Matters that they seem to point unambiguously to underlying beliefs.

Magic heads, like that of Bran, are found in other Indo-European contexts: what is not found elsewhere is the notion of reciprocal beheading, of which we have two striking instances. One, admittedly late, is found in the fourteenth-century *Gawain and the Green Knight*. The other, in 'Bricriu's Feast,' is eighth century. In the first, the Green Knight arrives, axe in hand, during the New Years festivities at King Arthur's court and challenges the guests to strike off his head, the only proviso being that the following year he will behead the striker. Sir Gawain alone accepts and cuts off the Green Knight's head, which he then picks up and takes away with him.

In due course, Gawain ventures forth to offer himself and is accommodated at the castle near where his rendezvous with the Green Knight is to take place. His host's wife thrice makes attempts on Gawain's chastity. The first two are rebuffed and reported to his host, but at the third he accepts a gift: the woman's girdle, which, she promises him, will protect his life. This he keeps secret.

When they meet, the Green Knight gives him three light taps on the neck, drawing blood only at the third. He then reveals himself as Gawain's host and explains that the two first strokes were because of his honesty in reporting the attempts to seduce him, each of which were instigated by the Green Knight himself as tests of his guest's virtue. The last blow is intended as a reproof for the fact that Gawain had kept secret the gift of the girdle.

In 'Bricriu's Feast,' the Ulster champions, unable to agree which of them deserves the Champion's Portion, submit their cause to the Druid Uath mac Imoman. He proposes a bargain: each of the contenders can cut of his head one day and the next day, he will cut off theirs. Two of them refuse; only Cu Chulainn accepts and slices off Uath's head, whereupon, like the Green Knight, Uath rises and carries his head back to his lake home

Next day Cu Chulainn appears to keep his side of the bargain. Again the blade falls three times, but at each it reverses itself before touching his neck, confirming that he is the one who deserves the Champion's Portion.

In both cases the climax takes place at a site associated with water – beside a lake for Cu Chulainn, a barrow beside a stream for Gawain. In the 1940s fourteen skulls of humans aged between twenty-five and thirty were recovered from an underground pool in the River Axe at Wookey Hole in Somerset, and there have been similar finds.

The fact that in both versions the incidents occur at New Year – Samain in the Irish one – is another significant point. The Green Knight can also be taken as another appearance of Cernunnos, the colour of his costume associating him with his forest habitat. If, as seems probable, this story and the incident in 'Bricriu's Feast' are related, then it would suggest that Imoman, too, is Cernunnos.

Another recurrent motif is that of pregnancy caused by the ingestion of an alien substance.

Thus, Etain Echrade, wife of Mider, transmogrified into a fly by the spell of Fuamnach, is swept out to sea by a tempest the magician has raised.

Battered, exhausted, more dead than alive, she falls through the smoke hole of the house of the Ulster chieftain Etar and into a drinking-cup. Etar's wife, suddenly thirsty, goes to fetch herself beer, pours it into the drinking-cup and with it swallows Etain who, in due course, is reborn.

After drinking an unspecified liquid, Dechtine has the dream in which Lugh tells her she is expecting his child. The two magical swineherds of the *Tain* undergo a series of shape-shifts to end up as two maggots. One falls into the river Cronn in Cuailnge, where it is swallowed by a cow belonging to Daire mac Fiachna while drinking and is reborn as the Brown Bull of Cuailnge.

The young Gwyon Bach, trying to escape the wrath of Cerridwen after he has accidentally swallowed the magic elixir intended for her ugly son, undergoes a series of transformations, the last of which is as a grain of wheat which lies with others on a threshing-floor, However, Cerridwen turns herself into a black hen, pecks up the grain, becomes pregnant and Gwyon is reborn as Taliessin. The transformations undergone by the Irish bard Tuan mac Cairill culminate in his becoming a salmon which, eaten by the wife of Cairill, causes his rebirth as Tuan.

The conclusion is obvious. At the time the original versions came into existence the causal link between sexual intercourse and conception had not been made. Without this link sexual relationships tend to be what we would term casual and promiscuous. That this was so among the Celts is confirmed by the impressions of outsiders and by hints, especially in the Irish stories, of comparatively relaxed sexual mores. For example, the Mebd's apparent nymphomania and Cu Chulainn's infatuation with Fand. But Celtic society was also matrilineal. Children took their mother's names, so that Tuan takes the name of his mother, Cairill, and the Ulster king is called Conchobhar mac Nessa, Nessa being his mother. The practice may well have been necessary because paternity was rarely certain.

By the late date at which the myths came to be written the Celts were in full possession of the biological facts. As a result, the storytellers often felt obliged to modify their material to accommodate the new knowledge Sometimes, as in 'The Birth of Cu Chulainn,' such interference is obvious by the damage done to the internal logic of the narrative. The original of the 'Birth' must have belonged to an epoch when pregnancy was regarded as a quasi-magical process. But, as the storyteller realises, most of Dechtine's fellows would have been more likely to attribute her condition to the usual cause. They may even had suspected her father, King Conchobhar, to have been responsible because of his habit of sharing her bed.

The traditional way of overcoming the embarrassment of having a daughter in such a predicament is to marry her off. Lugh is not available as a bridegroom, so the alternative is Sualdam. Dechtine's betrothal to Sualdam is likely to have been in the original, for the later incident of his disembodied head rousing the Ulstermen is plainly archaic, while examples of women pregnant by a god who still marry mortals are not lacking.

But knowledge about the process of conception would have altered attitudes towards such things, too. Respectable men do not usually marry women already made pregnant by some unknown predecessor. This difficulty is resolved by another interpolation: Dechtine's killing of the child in her womb by lying on it.

The unifying thread throughout is, however, that a line of mythical women are shown to give birth as a result of something they have devoured. To depreciate the role of the female is fully in accord with the Druids' shamanistic character. Before the reproductive process was understood the female magic of bringing about new life seemed to make her the collaborator with the Great Earth Mother, especially when she also became the planter and, therefore, producer of the new life from the soil itself.

To the shaman, she was an obvious rival, and, as I have tried to explain in my book on the subject,[14] I believe this makes understandable the antipathy to witchcraft – always ruled by the Great Earth Mother – among all the male-oriented belief-systems, of which shamanism, with its roots among the male hunters, was one.

There is one passage in the myths that helps to unite such disparate motifs as the Other World boar and the magical cauldron.

The episode of the Castle of the Golden Bowl in 'Manawydan' involves the disappearance of Pryderi and his mother Rhiannon; the disappearance of young males three days after birth also occurs in 'Pwyll' and 'Kulhwch.' It is true that Pryderi is not a baby, and it was at three days old that Celtic children were sent to their fosterers. What is more, Teirnon Twrvliant, the finder of Rhiannon's lost infant, is the sort of solid local yeoman who might well have been chosen as an adoptive father. On the other hand, Mabon and Pryderi's imprisonment in 'Kulhwch' bring to mind the young gods of vegetation myth, such as the Semitic Dummuzi or the Egyptian Osiris, who are taken into the underworld. The golden bowl (another cauldron?) is manifestly the sun symbol usually found in such myths, as is the underworld lord and his castle. Typically, too, rescue comes through a devoted woman who may be mother, wife or lover, sometimes a combination of all three. And as in the Adonis legend, the god's death or abduction takes place during a boar-hunt.

And is there a hint of the Castle of the Golden Bowl in the Mabon of 'Kulhwch,' whose full name is given as 'Mabon ap Modron' or 'Son, son of Mother'? The use of a common noun to denote a particular person makes sense only if the reference is understood, as when a Christian speaks of 'the Son,' or a devout Catholic refers to Mary as 'the Mother.' Modron is plainly not any mother. She is a mother in the same sense as Isis is mother – and saviour – of Osiris; that to say, she is a Great Mother.

14 *Shamanism: The Foundations of Magic* (Aquarian Press, 1986).

If we can establish that the Modron of 'Kulhwch' is the Rhiannon of 'Manawydan' we have also established that 'Mabon' is 'Pryderi.' Idris Foster, among others, has shown that Modron is the Welsh Morgan (the Morgan le Fay of the Arthurian Legends) and is, of course, the Irish Morrigan; others have demonstrated that the Morrigan is another form of Rhiannon (both mean 'The Great Queen'). It may appear difficult to reconcile the Rhiannon of the 'Pwyll' and 'Manawydan' with the harridan of 'Da Derga's Hostel'; but goddesses whose characters possess such contradictory aspects are common in Celticism – as Morgan le Fay demonstrates in the Arthurian stories. In any case, Rhiannon was the cause of the cruel joke played on her former lover, Gwawl.

That Mabon was the object of a widespread cult is shown by the occurrence of the name in Scotland, Wales, and Gaul. It is commemorated in two Scottish placenames: Lochmaben in Dumfriesshire and Clochmabenstane near Annan. He is also invoked under the name of 'Maponus' in five dedications in Northumberland, Lancashire, and Cumberland, in four of which he is equated with Apollo.[15] A document connected with the abbey of Savigny in central France, dated to about 1090, refers to *de Mabono fonte,* the fount or fountain of Mabon. He survived into Christian times and is commemorated in Wales as 'St.' Mabon, builder of the church at Llanfabon ('Fabon' is a mutative form of the name) in the parish of that name on the eastern border of Glamorganshire.

But if he is not Pryderi, is he even Mabon, or was Mabon, as Tolstoy believes, really an honorific for Lugh? Is he then the Young Son of the Mother? Not if we take the evidence of his mother's name as it occurs in 'Math,' for this names her as Arianrhod. On the other hand, it is Rhiannon who is cited as Lugh's mother in the Triads, and if this were so it would obviously complete the equation between Mabon and Lugh. And there are other dues pointing towards Rhiannon as Lugh's mother.

If the prisoner in the Castle of the Golden Bowl is Lugh, his release is probably connected with Lugnasad, his feast. This fell in early August and survived to become successively the Christian feast of Lammas and then the British August Bank Holiday. At Lammas, loaves made from the first ripe grain were taken to church and blessed. This overlays a similar pagan custom. In Manx folklore, early August was the time when Lugh struggled with and defeated Crom Dubh, thereby assuring the success of the corn harvest. In some parts of Ireland Lugnasad coincided with the festivals of two feminine deities; in one it was Carman, in the other Tailtiu (the name is commemorated in the placename Telltown), said to have been Lugh's foster-mother. Both, like Lammas and the Manx Lugnasad, connect the

---

15 This has fuelled speculation about Apollo's British genesis. The countless attempts to identify this profoundly mysterious god have included those which claim to derive his name from the word 'Apple' via the Welsh *aval.*

feast and the god in whose honour it was held with the fruits of the earth. Two things link Rhiannon, like the feminine figures of the classical vegetation myth, with the fertility of the soil. First, her equine character. With this in mind, consider Gerald's account of the newly appointed king's ritual marriage to a white mare. The animal represents – indeed, in the act of sacrifice, actually *becomes* – the territorial goddess, the deity upon whose goodwill all fruitfulness is dependent. This would account for the fact that the underground silos at Danebury hill-fort, which had been used to store grain, had horses' heads in them.

The conclusion is that, according to Celtic vegetation-myth of which we have relics in the episode of the Castle of the Golden Bowl, a young god descends into the underworld to procure for his people the gift of growing corn. He is assisted by his mother who is, in fact, a divine mare, which is why, while a prisoner, she is actually treated as a beast of burden.

Further corroboration of the character of the Golden Bowl episode as a vegetation myth is suggested by the mouse-motif. The one Manawydan catches comes from a plague of the creatures so great that 'neither number nor measure could be set on it.' Their depredations have left Manawydan's corn-fields bare – that is to say, in exactly the condition which befalls land denied the fecund influence of the vegetation-god. It will return to fruitfulness only when he is freed. And just such a deliverance comes about in the next few lines.

The Celts present a paradox: that of a people, temperamentally incapable of the sustained cooperation necessary to transform themselves from a loose tribal federation into a nation, but which, nonetheless, exhibit a consistency of religious belief, a devotion to it and a readiness to detect divine influence in all life's activities which is lacking among those contemporaries who had succeeded in unifying themselves.

In the most famous account of the struggle for Troy, Homer's *Iliad*, gods are involved. Though they sometimes use their power to assist one hero or another, often at critical moments they will abandon him and, without hint of remorse, allow him to pass into the world of dusty shadows which was the Homeric afterlife. If there is any noteworthy characteristic about the Homeric gods it is, not just that they are above the struggles and sufferings of petty mortals, but that their actions are accountable only in terms of their relations with one another. The Ulster Cycle has been called an 'Irish Iliad,' and there are certainly parallels. In both cases, the cause of war is an abduction, in the one of a woman, in the other of a bull. Much of the narrative of both is taken up with the description of the single combats of heroes.

It is now generally agreed that the Trojan Wars actually took place, and it is equally possible that a real war between Ulster and Connaught is commemorated in the Ulster cycle of stories. What we do not get in the Greek epic as we do in the Irish, is any sense of a historical struggle elevated to a spiritual one – as when the ford where Cu Chulainn slays all his enemies becomes a symbol for the junction between two worlds.

The Hindu epic, *The Ramayana,* exhibits the same sense of spiritual conflict, between good and evil or, more precisely, between light and darkness. In fact, it was the presence of this quality in the Celtic myths that facilitated their conversion into Christian allegories – for instance, the figure of the Arthurian knight, the Galahad, *mens sana in corpore sano,* involved in lifelong struggle with evil.

As we have seen, Brahminism and Druidism lay close to shamanism and both saw the supernatural as penetrating and embracing every aspect of life. The deities of Irish and Welsh myth mix freely and equally with the race of mortals, sometimes they even marry into it. In this respect, they are less like the gods of Greek myth than the fairies, pixies, and goblins of children's stories, the Pucks whom Elizabethan peasants blamed for all sorts of misfortunes and who could, if suitably bribed, assist the maid or housewife with her chores.

Indeed, these are the true descendants of Celtic gods, like the Tuatha De Danann. Rhys tells countless stories derived from the Welsh folk-memory of women who had wandered into the lives of bachelors and widowers, just as Macha wanders into the life of the Ulster widower Crunniac. When a *geis* on them is broken they return to the lakes from which they came, sometimes followed there by distraught spouses.

Since the Other World lies so close to our own – there were gods, rather than fairies, at the bottom of the Celtic garden – it is necessary only to visit a suitably charged spot like a burial mound, to follow the trail of a white boar, to throw water over a particular stone to find oneself in it.

The Celtic Other World, like the shaman's, is that of the dead. In 'Gereint and Enid,' the knight who appears in response to Enid's first scream is called Death, and when a knight with couched lance bears down on them she shouts to him: 'What fame can you win by *killing a dead man?*' The road along which they travel with the Little King divides and they must choose which to take. Forked ways in the Land of the Dead are to be found in the Mystery Religions and were known to the Pythagoreans in the fifth century bc. In another story, Peredur is faced by the same choice.

The road they take leads them to the games arena with its hedge of mist and its grim *cheveux de frise,* each of whose spikes, save two, carries a head. The implication is that the vacant ones are for the heads of Gereint and his companion. There is also the red brocade of the pavilion – red being the Celtic death-hue – while the horn which Gereint is to sound to bring the dreadful games to an end hangs from an appletree Gereint, like Peredur, returns from his Other World adventure; returns, that is to say, from one kind of reality to another, more familiar one. These are not simply isolated incidents: they are the very stuff of the Celtic world.

Chapter 11

HEIRS OF AN 'ANCIENT WISDOM'?

Over the preceding pages we have established that, outside of the few brief and partisan classical references, it is the myths that provide us with our largest fund of information about Druidism – though it is not altogether surprising that this should be so, since they were originally created to reflect a Druidic image of the supernatural and the human response to it.

Attitudes towards the Druids vary wildly. For some, they are a subject for uncritical adulation. Their more dubious practices, like human sacrifice, are ascribed either to the slander of enemies, to modern misunderstanding, or, if it is accepted that it took place at all, it is implied that the Druids were present only out of a reluctant duty, much as one imagines the more humane ecclesiastics might have attended an *auto-da-fé*.

One by-product of admiration has been the attempt to revive what was conceived to be Druidic belief and practice. On flimsy evidence tricked out by imagination, Druidic doctrine is rehashed and totally specious rites, such as the bardic Gorsedds and, later, the Stonehenge summer-solstice ceremony, enacted. There are even 'Druidic' costumes, which range from something resembling the uniform of a 1930s nanny to normal dress topped off with a Victorian smoking-cap.

At the opposite extreme are those who, *à la* Tierney, see the Druids as little better than jujumen, battening on the superstition of the ignorant and indulging in the sort of barbaric practices mentioned by Caesar. At the same time, their followers, the Celts at large, were nailing the heads of slain enemies to the porches of their houses or embalming them to show off to visitors, much as one might show off a collection of first editions.

Into the second category comes Kendrick, whose study (first published in 1927) is still a standard reference work. It has little to tell us, apart from how deficient our knowledge is and how dubious is the moiety we possess. Nothing much has changed in half a century, for Piggott is in much the same vein, citing Kendrick with approval. He questions whether Diviciacus the Aeduan chief, probably himself a Druid and who so impressed Cicero, was able to speak adequate Latin and, at one point, whether Celtic society itself was more than 'conditionally' literate.

These contemporary attitudes so exactly match those of classical antiquity that it is as if each party had deliberately allied itself to one or other of the earlier schools of thought. For Caesar, Tacitus, and Lucan, Rome was the deliverer of the wretched Celts from the excesses of the Druids. To others, like Posidonius and Strabo, the Druids were sages of transcendant wisdom. Then, as now, each side, in its desire to make good its case, selects the evidence that suits it.

It is true that most of the classical writers who mention the Druids favourably lived at a time when they were no longer easily to be found, certainly by Greek or Roman. It is also true they can sometimes allow pro-Druidic bias to run away with them. At the same time, most of their detractors just as certainly never encountered a Druid face to face either. In these circumstances, it is a question of examining the available testimony and, as it is not always possible to distinguish fact from wishful thinking, trying to arrive at a likely conclusion on a balance of probabilities.

Distressing as it may be to their advocates, we have to acknowledge that the Celts, as a whole, did practise head-hunting and used their trophies for household decoration. That decapitation played some kind of ritual role is plain from the myths, which means we can probably accept that its inspirers were the Druids. There are solid reasons for accepting that they carried out divination from the anguished writhing of those they had stabbed and that they practised human sacrifice.

Even if we treat the Roman witnesses as hostile, we still have the Irish missionaries. A poem in the Books of Leinster, Lecan, and Ballymote and in the Rennes *Dindsenchas* records the sacrifice at Samain of one-third of the first-born to a stone idol called 'Crom Cruaich,' which stood at Mag Sleacht in Co. Cavan. The last two verses of the poem describe the destruction of the idols by St. Patrick. There is also the evidence that Lindow Man was a sacrificial victim.

Just as there is no evidence the Druids relished these activities, so there is none that they found them particularly abhorrent. Yet, before reacting with horror and throwing our support, as history has done, on the side of Caesar and Tacitus, we have to recognise that human sacrifice had been banned in Rome only at the beginning of the century in which these commentators were born, while slaughter on a massive scale was still being practised in the Roman circus in their lifetimes for the purely frivolous purpose of entertaining the crowd. One such 'entertainment' sponsored by Caesar himself involved a huge naval battle in which hundreds were killed, maimed, and drowned. At least the Druids could claim the sanction of religion.

In any case, that practices repugnant to ourselves can subsist beside what we acknowledge as authentic knowledge is shown by the pre-Columbian civilisations of the Americas. A famous frieze discovered on a Mayan site in southern Mexico in 1946 shows, in a series of tableaux, a raid on a neighbouring people for sacrificial victims, their presentation to the king, and finally their immolation. Yet the Maya were master mathematicians, astronomers, and calendarists. We shall never now be able to judge the full extent of their knowledge since, in an act of vandalism unparalleled since the Islamic destruction of the library of Alexandria in AD 300, Bishop Diego de Landa ordered the burning of all Mayan books, 'as they contained nothing in which there were not to be seen superstition and the lies of the devil.' Fortunately not all the Church's representatives behaved with such high-handedness or our ignorance of the pre-Columbian civilisations would be total. There were also those Franciscan monks who, while deploring human sacrifice, recognised the many estimable qualities of those in their pastoral charge.

Not dissimilar to the more enlightened Franciscan missionaries in Latin America were those who went to Ireland in the fifth century. Of Druidic knowledge they tell us nothing, perhaps because they were unimpressed with it. Or it may have been because they did not see it as much affecting their own sphere of activity – the conversion of the heathen.

There is at least one strong hint that the Church itself saw the Druids as an intellectual force to be reckoned with. Far from being renowned for learning, it was more often the ignorance of monks that was proverbial. Yet the missionaries of Ireland were to acquire an international reputation for scholarship, making them a potent influence in the western Church. Dillon believes this may have been due to the fact that it had become a place of refuge for learned Christians fleeing barbarian invaders on the Continent. But in choosing Ireland they must have regarded it as a congenial environment, a place where they would be among mental equals. The implication is that the missionaries sent to the island in the first place had been specially selected for their ability to match those with whom they had to compete in the struggle for souls, just like the Jesuits in a later age.

Matching may have gone further. There is evidence to suggest that some of the missionaries tried to make themselves as much like Druids as possible, perhaps even adopting the Druidic tonsure, for the question was later to become a bone of contention between the Celtic and Roman Churches. Celtic monks were accused of adopting 'the tonsure of Simon Magus.' Simon Magus, more correctly 'Simon the Magus,' was the magician denounced in the Book of Acts, but his name was invariably invoked to describe anyone who indulged in what the Church regarded as magical practices and elsewhere the Druids are specifically accused of committing the 'sin of the Simon Magus.' This makes it likely that the tonsure involved was in fact the Druidic one. The missionaries also undertook the care of the sick and the running of hospitals, for which previously the Druids had been responsible.

I suggest, therefore, that there is sufficient evidence to justify us in looking more closely at Druidic knowledge. One place we might begin doing so is in Caesar, who, as we have seen, had strong reasons for showing the Druids in an uncomplimentary light. His statement that their training took twenty years has never seriously been questioned and the name Bangor, which survives as the name of a Welsh and a Northern Irish town, commemorates the existence within them of Druidic colleges.

He also mentions the Druidic predilection for 'long discussions about the heavenly bodies and their movements,' which implies an involvement with astronomy and brings us a little closer to the statement Cicero made – in connection with the visit to Rome of the Aeduan Diviciacus – that the Druids possessed knowledge comparable with what the Greeks called *Physiologia*. Central to *Physiologia* was astronomy – actually synonymous with astrology.

Cicero is not easily dismissed. He had been educated at the Platonic Academy in Athens and was as much at home in Greek as in his native tongue. If Diviciacus's address to the Roman senate had amounted to no more than vapourings in dog-Latin it is hardly likely that he, of all people, would have been taken in.

While it is true that most of the classical writers who mention the Druids favourably lived at a time when distance had begun to lend enchantment to the view, others were closer to them. Undeniably the greatest of all experts on the Celts was Posidonius, who in his youth had travelled extensively in the Celtic lands. At the end of a distinguished academic career he had gone to live in retirement on the island of Rhodes, where Cicero visited him.

To be sure, Posidonius may well have been looking for support for his own Stoic philosophy which, believing in the enervating effects of civilisation, was only too eager to convert the Celts and their Druids into Noble Savages. He was, none the less, a man of extraordinary knowledge and versatility. Besides being a philosopher, he was a historian, scientist, astronomer, and a geographer of such eminence that he provided Columbus with the stimulus for his voyages of discovery sixteen centuries later. It is therefore unlikely he would have mistaken hocus-pocus for genuine knowledge.

Another who saw Druidism in action was the Elder Pliny, and so, if we are to take him at his word, did Pomponius Meta. But there is an earlier witness than any of these. Hecateus of Abdera (c. 500 BC) was, like Posidonius, widely travelled. He plainly had a high opinion of the Druids for, according to him, Pythagoras's instructor, Abaris, was one of them.

It is, in fact, perfectly likely that Pythagoras visited Gaul and possibly the British Isles, though there are other and more plausible sources for the ideas he was later to develop. But the truth or otherwise of Hecateus's assertion is immaterial. What is significant is that he, an educated Milesian, living at a time when Druidism was flourishing, can actually credit it with providing the philosophical ground base for a thinker who had lived only shortly before his own lifetime, who commanded the most enormous respect, and who was to help shape the philosophies of Socrates, Plato, and Aristotle. There were far more obvious choices for the role. One would have been the Thracian caste of wise men, the *kapnobatai,* from which the prophet Orpheus, whose ideas we know to have influenced Pythagoras, probably came.

Diogenes Laertius in *The Lives and Opinions of the Eminent Philosophers* brackets the Druids with the Persian Magi, with what he calls the 'Chaldeans' – in fact the Babylonic priesthood – and with an Indian sect whom he describes as the 'Gymnosophists.' Diogenes flourished in the middle of the third century AD, making him an extremely late source; but he was citing two now lost works, one by Sotion of Alexander and the other by Aristotle, who lived in the fourth century BC.

The Babylonic priesthood, successors of the Sumerians, were men of internationally acknowledged learning, some of whose contributions to astronomy and mathematics are still with us. The Persian Magi enjoyed a similar reputation. By tradition, though the gospel does not say so, they were the 'wise men from the East' who, recognising the Bethlehem star, went to visit the Christ-child. (Pliny, we recall, mentions the Magi in conjunction with the Druids.)

On Diogenes's list we also have the *Gymnosophists.* They have been identified as the *Muni,* the predecessors of the Yogi, and the Greek name for them, which means 'Naked Wise Men,' would seem appropriate enough for these loin-cloth wearing figures. However, Strabo calls them Brahmins. They first began to emerge in India in Vedic times – that is to say, between 1500–1200 BC. Their prestige was based on belief in their ritual purity and scholarship.

Like the Magi and the Babylonic priesthood, their contribution to knowledge has been formidable. In mathematics, for instance, the concept of zero is attributed to them. We have already examined some of the many similarities between the Druids and Brahmins. Since the credentials of the other three can be established, it would at least be odd if the only cuckoo in the nest were the Druids, particularly as there was no lack of alternative candidates for inclusion in Diogenes's list.

Thus, on balance, there is just as much reason for believing in the reality of Druidic knowledge as for rejecting it.

What, then, was this knowledge? In view of the secrecy surrounding Druidic teachings we can do little more than conjecture.

The esteem in which the *Aes Dana* were held is indicative of the Celts' reverence for poetry, science, and technology, and we know they worked first bronze, then iron, and that they practised enamelling and possessed considerable craft skill.

Cicero's statement about Druidic 'Physiologia,' Caesar's on their discussions about the heavenly bodies, as well as the Coligny calendar, are testimony to a preoccupation with astronomy. This is further confirmed by the existence of Celtic names for many of the constellations, so that besides the 'Caer Arianrhod,' mentioned earlier, we have Caer Gwydion for the Milky Way and Llys Don (The Court of Don or Dana) for Cassiopeia. Indeed, if the Coligny calendar was the Druids' unaided work – and nothing that might have provided a model has ever been found – they possessed astronomical, calendrical, and mathematical skills of a high order.

Geoffrey of Monmouth mentions a 'college of two hundred learned men, skilled in astronomy and other arts' which existed at Caerleon on Usk in the time of Arthur and which was apparently under royal patronage. He may well have been recapitulating legends about a Druidic bangor that had once existed in the town. Taliessin's boast that 'I know the names of the stars from north to south' is a hint that, with other Druidic functions, astronomy had in his time – the sixth century – become part of the bard's. This would be consistent with Triad 89 where the 'three renowned astronomers of the Island of Britain' are listed as Idris the giant, Gwydion ap Don, and Gwynn ap Nudd. 'Such was their knowledge of the stars, their natures and qualities,' it says, 'that they were able to predict whatever they desired to be known until the Day of Doom.' The giant Idris is a legendary figure associated with Mount Snowdon, which is also known as Cadeir Idris, 'The Seat of Idris'; high places are, of course, often chosen by astronomers for their observations.

Astronomical knowledge leads to the question of the Druids and Stonehenge. Though still debated, the evidence that it and some of the other stone circles served the dual purpose of ritual centre and astronomical computer is now taken seriously. In other words, the builders of Stonehenge and the other henges and stone circles belonged to unknown Stone Age civilisation with a highly developed astronomy. Were the Druids acquainted with it?

The Stonehenge area was the site of the Bronze Age Wessex Culture. While its citizens cannot have been involved in the original building, they may have added the outer ring of blue stones and used it for its original purpose. Grave goods indicate a trading partnership between the Wessex Culture and Mycenae, as well as other Aegean civilisations, which at one time led to the belief that it had been founded by migrants from those cultures. Among competing theories is that they were an early wave of Celtic settlers. On the other hand, if we assume that the Celts began to arrive around 800 BC, then the Wessex Culture had by then virtually ceased to exist. There is certainly no direct evidence to associate the Druids with

Stonehenge, though an incident in which Celtic nobles were said to have been treacherously slain by the Saxons during a banquet has been tentatively located there, largely on the evidence of Triad 21, which in fact says only that it took place on Salisbury Plain.

However, the Druids could have realised, if only from local legend, that Stonehenge lay in a region that had witnessed an epoch of past greatness and that the stone circle itself served an astronomical purpose. We have seen how the Celts who came to Britain adopted local practices such as shaft burial. Imitation bespeaks admiration and admiration must have been inspired by what they found – just as what the Romans found when they conquered Greece inspired *them* to emulation.

Hecateus of Abdera has already been cited as describing Abaris, the legendary instructor of Pythagoras, as a Druid. In another passage, repeated by Diodorus, he mentions an island, no smaller than Diodorus's native Sicily, which lay opposite Gaul and which can be plainly identified as Britain. It was inhabited, he says, by 'Hyperboreans.' The Hyperboreans were a mythical people said to come from 'beyond the North Wind,' the last survivors of Hesiod's Golden Age, who lived happy and virtuous thousand-year lives. They accorded special veneration to Apollo who, in Greek mythology was said to have been a Hyperborean himself and to return to his people annually.[16] As a mark of their devotion Hecateus's insular Hyperboreans had erected a sacred enclosure. It took the form of 'a magnificent circular temple adorned with many rich offerings' and is usually assumed to be either Stonehenge or Woodhenge. So close were their relations with the sun-god that he visited them every nineteen years, his presence among them being celebrated with dancing and music.

The reference to nineteen years is significant as this is the period of the Metonic cycle, named after the Greek astronomer Meton, who used it as a means of bringing lunar and solar years into synchronicity. Nineteen years is roughly the period between one eclipse and another (it is actually 18 years, 11 1/3 days). Professor Fred Hoyle has shown that the so-called Aubrey Holes at Stonehenge, the circle of fifty-six pits outside the trilithons, may have been designed for eclipse prediction by using a system of markers and, though the movement of these is quite complex, they could have operated with considerable accuracy. Furthermore, this may well explain Apollo's nineteen-year incarnations, for if the period is that between eclipses, what could be more logical – the sun being absent from the sky – than that it was because its ruling deity was visiting his earthly worshippers?

But the Coligny calendar – the key archaeological evidence of Druidic astronomy – is also based on the nineteen-year or Metonic cycle and, as

16 As we have seen, there have been numerous attempts to prove that Apollo was British – by no means all of them coming from British sources!

Piggott points out, it may well have been that the training course, which Caesar says lasted twenty years, actually lasted nineteen, thus corresponding with the Druid's epoch.

The Metonic cycle connects the Druids with the Babylonians, also on Diogenes's list. These were the greatest of all astronomers of the Ancient World. If we were dependent on this alone it could be dismissed as being due to the fact that more than one people had realised that one effect of an eclipse was to realign sun and moon. However, there is another, if more tenuous connection. Markale points out that the method of counting still used by the French – which, though their language possesses words for a hundred, a thousand, etc., actually only goes up to sixty and lacks words for seventy, eighty, and ninety – is a Celtic survival. Since a similar system is used by the Welsh, he is no doubt right. (In Welsh, eighty is 'pedwar ugain,' four twenties, just as in French it is 'quatre-vingts.') Like the French and the Welsh, the Mesopotamians had words for a hundred and a thousand, but also used sixty as their main base, a fact commemorated in our sixty-second minute and sixty-minute hour.

In other words, as well as having intimations of a link between the Druids and the other members of Diogenes's list, we also have circumstantial evidence of a Druidic involvement in an activity attributed to them – namely, astronomy. This could well account for their inclusion in the list and, if the British Druids were using the stone circles for the purpose for which they had been built, it would also help to account for Caesar's statement (supported in the Irish myths) that British Druidism was regarded as the most highly developed and, hence, that Britain was the place to which all who wanted to advance their studies came.

In the light of this one might well reconsider the question of Hecateus's British Hyperboreans. These mysterious people occur in a number of Greek references. They are not only the survivors of the Golden Age, they are also the heirs and custodians of its wisdom, which, it is plain, is largely of an esoteric and magical kind. It was to their land beyond the North Wind that, accompanied by Athena, Perseus went in search of the mythical gorgon Medusa and where he found, slew, and decapitated her, taking her head as proof of his deed.

Perseus was connected with Thessaly, which was the centre of a Hyperborean cult, and the fifth-century poet Pindar makes use of the fact in his Pythian Ode X dedicated to the winner of the boys' double foot-race at the Pythian Games. These, sacred to Apollo, were also connected with the Hyperboreans and took place at Delphi every four years. On this particular occasion the winner happened to have been a native of Thessaly, thus strengthening the link.

In the poem, Pindar establishes the mystical character of the Hyperborean land and people which, he says, is never deserted by the Muse, where everywhere girls are dancing, and the sounds of harp and flutes are ever to be heard. Its people bind their hair with gilded bay leaves, know neither sickness nor old age, and instead of toiling or fighting wars pass their time in feasting.

These characteristics are shared by the Celtic Other World, according to Taliessin *Spoils of Annwvyn*. Here, too, old age and sickness are unknown; there is music and marvellous drink. But for Pindar, too, the Hyperborean's land is in the Other World for he warns that 'the marvellous road to the games of the People beyond the North' is not to be reached in ships or on foot.

Apparently undeterred by Pindar, at least one Greek traveller – Aristeas of Proconnesus – set out to find it. Actually a distinction needs to be made here. The Greeks – models of precision in so many ways – used the word 'Hyperborean' extremely loosely. Sometimes they appear to mean a group of gods or, at any rate, of Other World beings; in others, they mean their physical worshippers. (The Celtic myths suggest a similar looseness in regard to the Tuatha De Danann. Sometimes they seem to be physical inhabitants of Ireland before the Milesians arrival; in others, divinities.)

Pindar was using the word in the first sense and Aristeas in the second. He was seeking the land inhabited by the worshippers of the Hyperborean gods and he was doing so because of the wisdom they had acquired, presumably because of a special relationship between themselves and their deities.

His journey took him north-eastwards, to Scythia, where he was admonished to go no further but was told that the Hyperborean land lay beyond gold-bearing mountains – which must be those of the Altaic Range.

Here, indeed, is a realm of high magic. It is from the peoples living there that we get the word 'shaman' – and surely if anyone can claim to have a special relationship with the divine it is the shaman. It is the region of the Bon magicians who helped to shape Chinese Taoism and Hindu Tantrism as well as Tibetan Buddhism, and within it stands the sacred Mount Meru, dwelling place of the Seven Sages, mentioned in the *Rig Veda*. It is a Great Centre in the sense discussed earlier, a place where our own world and the Other World meet. Indeed, Mount Meru is actually called 'The Centre of the World.'

From the account of Aristeas's journey two significant points emerge. The first is that it shows that the Scythians, whose influence on the Celts has already been noted, had, like the Greeks, preserved a legend of the Hyperboreans. The second is that, though the Hyperboreans have been equated with everyone from the Libyans to the Chinese – including, as we saw, the British – this area corresponds more closely with the modern attempts to locate them, including that of Geoffrey Ashe in *The Ancient*

Wisdom. As Ashe points out, there is evidence for the existence of a body of knowledge, later diffused, originating in the Altaic zone. It may well have included astronomy and mathematics. Among possible beneficiaries were the Mesopotamian, the Hindus, and the Persians – that is to say, three out of the four on Diogenes's list. It excludes only the Druids.

Of course, we still have Hecateus's Hyperboreans living on their island opposite Gaul; but Aristeas's journey, and studies like Geoffrey Ashe's would seem to rule them out, certainly as the original Hyperboreans. On the other hand, it is just possible, if they are an actual as opposed to an Other World people, that those in Britain could have been a migrating group who preceded the Celts in the British Isles and perhaps even built Stonehenge.

There is one more thing to be said. Accounts of the Hyperboreans bring to mind not only Taliessin's Other World and the Celtic Islands of the Blessed, but also the stories of the Tuatha De Danann. Of their arrival in Ireland we have three differing accounts. In the first, and probably the oldest, they 'came out of the skies,' a version which has been enthusiastically pounced on by those who believe in sporadic interventions in earthly affairs by extraterrestrials; more probably it means we are to regard them as divinities. In another, their homeland was said to be in 'the southern isles of the world.' This is Robert Graves's preferred location, and in *The White Goddess* he equates them with the Danaans and deduces that Tuathan knowledge came from the Mediterranean. However, interestingly enough, a third account has them coming – like the Hyperboreans – from the north.

Two things are clear. One is that, insofar as the mythology gives us any hints of the sources of Druidic knowledge, it is the Tuatha De Danann who are credited with imparting it. The other is that they were already in occupation at the time of the Celtic invasion under Mile and it was the Milesians who gave them the name of 'Tuatha De Danann,' the People of the Goddess Dana. The incidence of river names like Danube, Don, Dniepr, and Dniestr suggests that the Celts had a feminine deity with a similar name, though, if we go by the myths, her cult can never have been of great importance for she occurs in them only as part of the name of other characters, so that the smith-god Govannon, for example, is called, in full, Govannon son of Don. She herself never appears.

A little interpretation is surely justified. The Milesians, on their arrival on Irish shores, found an existing population practising agriculture, perhaps metal-working, but, at any rate, more advanced than the newcomers in signficant ways. After the custom of agriculturists, the religious practice of the autochthonous people centred on an Earth Mother. Whatever her original name may have been, the invaders equated her with one of their own whom they called Danu or Dana, in much the same way as the

Romans were later to equate Celtic gods with theirs. Accordingly the original inhabitants came to be called the 'Tuatha De Danann.'

Can we assume them, if not to have been a kind of outpost of the Hyperborean, to have had some kind of access to Hyperborean knowledge which they passed on to the Druids?

When the available information about the Hyperboreans and the Tuatha is placed side by side the correspondences are astonishing. To Pindar, the former are an Other World people connected with a northerly land. According to him, and to other references, they are the source of a wisdom which encompasses the magical. Stories of a similar people are to be found in Persian and Hindu mythologies, while there are hints that even the Mesopotamians believed in a gifted northern people.

The Tuathans are also an Other World people who possess extraordinary wisdom with a strongly magical tinge. In one version of the myth of their arrival in Ireland they are said to have come 'out of the skies'; in another, from the north. In any event, legends about the inhabitants of the British Isles reminded Hecateus of those of the Hyperboreans strongly enough for him to call them by that name, while Taliessin speaks of the Celtic Other World in terms almost exactly the same as those used by Pindar to describe the land of the Hyperboreans.

The Magi, the Brahmins, and the Babylonic priesthood can be shown to have connections with a northerly region which has been at least tentatively identified as the Altaic Zone, itself identified as the area from which the Hyperboreans and their god, Apollo, were said to have come. Just as it would be strange if the Druids were the only one of the four founders of philosophy who had no right to be on Diogenes's list, so it would be strange if they were the only ones who had no contact with Hyperborean knowledge.

I offer these conclusions without comment, but with the suggestion that, in one way or another, if such a thing as an 'Ancient Wisdom' ever existed, and whatever it may have comprised, the Druids may well have partaken of it. And, if this is so, it might explain a reputation for wisdom which led to their inclusion in a list of those who certainly deserved it.

PART III

MYTHS
AND THE
LATER
HISTORY
OF THE
CELTS

Chapter 12

THE ARTHURIAN CYCLE

It was ever the aim of Christian missionaries to present their religion, not as a breach with the past, but as its culmination. As St. Columba, the missionary to Scotland, was to put it, Christ was the new Druid.

The success of the policy in Ireland is reflected in a literary effusion, as impressive as anything that had gone before, which the encounter between paganism and the emissaries of the new religion produced. In stories of a deeply moving poignancy, gods and heroes reincarnate and play host to their Christian visitors who, in their turn, treat them with the greatest respect as men who 'carried truth in their hearts.' One of Finn's followers, Caoilte, was said to have lived long enough to have met St. Patrick himself and to have kept the saint enraptured with his stories before being received into the faith.

The twelfth-century Irish *Lebor na hUidre* contains the legend of Tuan mac Cairill. It tells how St. Finnen, a sixth-century abbot of Moville, Co. Donegal, went to visit an aged neighbouring chieftain. Refused entrance, the abbot sat down on his doorstep and fasted for an entire Sunday. The pagan custom of fasting 'against' anyone who had done an injustice has already been discussed and St. Finnen's employment of it makes it clear, that he understood its significance. It had the required effect for the old man was compelled to admit him, after which inauspicious beginning the two became firm friends and Tuan was a frequent visitor to the monastery. Asked about his name and lineage, Tuan embarked on the story of his successive lives during which he had witnessed all the major events in his island's history.

In another tale the beautiful Ethne, brought up in the court of the sea god, Manannan mac Lir and, hence, one of the Tuatha, loses her veil of invisibility after bathing with her friends. Unshielded from mortal gaze, she cannot return to the *sidh*, wanders disconsolately and, at length, finds herself in a monastery garden. The monk, who befriends her, receives her into both the Church and the community of humans.

A devout Christian from then on, Ethne still sometimes recalls her past with nostalgia. On one occasion while praying she hears a flurry about her and the distant voices of her old companions of the Tuatha, calling sadly for her. Soon after this she dies in the arms of St. Patrick.

No less touching is the story of the Swans of Fionuala. Jealous of the love of her husband Ur, father of Mananann, for his four children by a previous marriage, their sorceress-stepmother Aoife turns them into swans. They are to remain in this state for a total of nine hundred years until 'the woman of the south is mated with the man of the north.'

The eldest sister, Fionuala, does her best to act as substitute mother to the younger children, but they all suffer greatly through long cold winters and stormy seas. As the period of their suffering comes towards its end they plan to fly back to their father's old palace, but arrive to find only overgrown ruins.

While taking in this dismal scene they hear the pealing of a bell. At first startled, they approach and find a hermit's oratory where, though still in swan form, they are converted to the Faith.

In the meantime, the princess of Munster in the south of Ireland is to marry the chieftain of Connaught in the north. As her wedding gift she begs for four swans renowned for their grace and beauty. Hearing that the swans are in the hermit's cell, the Connaught prince goes to seek them and, when refused, tries to take them by force. It is the last act of the spell and before the eyes of pagan ruler and Christian monk they revert to their original form, not as radiant divinities, but as toothless, withered infinitely aged humans.

Horrified by the sight, the intruder flees while the hermit, realising that death could not long be delayed, administers baptism. With her last breath, Fionuala asks for them all to be buried enfolded in her arms, just as in the past she had protected them against the icy seas with her wings.

One of these stories make it plain that not everyone welcomed the gospel as Ethne or Fionuala had. In it we find Oisin mac Finn taking sanctuary in St. Patrick's monastery. A sad and disappointed old man, he contrasts the frugal refectory fare with the Fenian feasts, the emasculated monkish chanting with the lusty songs of the past. But what shocks him most is the notion of a God who could consign a man like Finn to Hell. On St. Patrick's argument that it is 'because he gave no heed of God,' he casts only scorn. 'Finn under locks? A heart without envy or hatred?' A God he could respect would be one who gave food and riches, refusing none, like Finn.

With Oisin growing older, Patrick labours for his conversion, contrasting Finn's miseries 'on the flagstones of pain' with the joys of heaven. But a heaven without his beloved dog, and where Finn and his Fenian companions are absent, has no attractions for Oisin. He can only repeat: 'Were God in bonds, Finn would fight to free him. Finn left none in pain or danger.' And, at the end of the story, he is still unreconciled.

Admirable as these transition tales may be, they do not, strictly speaking, represent a mythology. Rather than being 'collective dreams' they are the literary products of individuals. Some scholars, like Gerald Murphy, even suggest the story-cycles such as those in the *Acallam na Senorec,* The Colloquy of the Elders, were the work of a single hand.

A mythology as defined in Chapter 1 was to appear, not in Ireland, but in Britain. The Arthurian cycle, though shot through with relics of the past, was to all intents and purposes a new one.

It was so of necessity, because the situation which had called it into being was an entirely new one. One of the essential functions of myth is to provide a frame of reference to which every individual member of a society can attune his conduct. In the same way that every Christian is urged to model himself on the founder of his religion, the pagan Celt was expected to model himself on the heroes like Cu Chulainn.

It is for this reason that an agreed and uniformly accepted mythology is a prerequisite for every human society. It provides its essential cohesion, so that when a society, like our own, has no shared mythology it is in danger of disintegration or destruction by another society where it is still a dynamic force.

In the Irish stories we have the example of a people living in an heroic age, replete with self-confidence and unswerving in their belief in the superiority of their society and of the ideology that underpins it. The impressions conveyed by those of Arthur is quite different: it is one of yearning nostalgia. Yet, as certainly as any other mythology, it was fulfilling a unifying purpose. What it was is clear only in the context of the historical background.

One of the more mystifying aspects of Roman rule is how little and sporadic opposition to it was. In Gaul there had been the revolt of the young Avernian chieftain Vercingetorix. In Britain, Cassivelaunus, Boudicca, and Caratacus may have seen themselves as the defenders of tribal independence, but they were also struggling to maintain their own dynasties, in the last case a large and powerful one.

Indeed, far from opposing occupation, the reverse seems to be true, for, as we saw in Chapter 4, by the fifth century a large section of the British aristocracy regarded itself as consisting of the fully paid-up members of a Roman province. Naturally, lack of resistance was no accident, but part of a deliberate, two-pronged Roman policy of which one aspect had been the ruthless and brutal suppression of rebellion at the first spark and the other the creation of that very aristocracy.

Apparent inactivity should not lead us to suppose that opposition was non-existent. Such as there was came from two sources: the peasantry, always deeply traditionalist, and the old pre-Roman aristocracy. Tolstoy discusses the survival of Druidism among the realms of some of the more powerful of the North British kings. One of these was Urien who ruled Rheged and who was succeeded by his son Owein – the Owein or Yvain of Arthurian Legends.

To such men, those ennobled by the occupiers were regarded as a vulgar *parvenus,* a judgement which, from the indications of their ostentatious lifestyles, was not unmerited.

One may well suppose that, as has so often happened in history, one of the things which gave a new lease of life to Druidism was that it came to symbolise national independence. Centuries Later, when another Owein, Owein Glendwr, was fighting for Welsh independence, there was a similar revival of the past and Glendwr's 'magicians', with their Druidic ability to raise mist and storm, were blamed for the series of defeats inflicted on the forces of the English king, Henry IV.

The situation was exacerbated by the arrival in Britain of a competing religion – Christianity. To be sure, like Ireland, the country would have had its Oisins, able to make only adverse comparisons between their own and the new religion with its Passion, its Hell, its Purgatory, and its unsmiling God. Fatalistic Druidism might be given to practices like human sacrifice, yet it was ultimately optimistic. The joys of Tir na n'Og were the familiar, earthly, and earthy ones, while for the warrior who fell in battle there was the certainty of rebirth in mortal form and, with it, the return to all the boisterous joys of living. At the same time, Christianity must have been seen by many as yet another foreign imposition and a further source for antagonism towards the occupiers and their collaborators. However, as political realists, the traditionalists must have recognised that, while trying to preserve the past against the day when it could be re-established, for the present such resistance as they could offer must take a passive form.

Hope that the long awaited day of freedom might be dawning began in the closing decades of the fourth century AD. Its stimulus was the succession of Roman disasters which led to the systemic stripping of the British garrisons as the troops in them were required for more urgent tasks nearer home As each unit embarked, the stated intention was that it would be replaced as soon as the immediate crisis was over. Instead it deepened.

If the conservative element in British society had looked forward to these events eagerly, to the Romanised nobility they came as a considerable shock and were seen as acts of betrayal by those on whom they had come to rely. Some of their fears were soon to be realised and, in the realisation, showed the traditionalists that their troubles had not ended with the exit of the Romans. By 410, with the country left virtually unprotected, the Scottish and Pictish raids which, even at full strength, the legionaries had been unable totally to prevent, became ever more daring. Very soon there was the added misery of incursions from across the North Sea. In 446 an impassioned plea for Roman aid was made. Unable to provide it, the emperor gave permission for the organisation of local defence forces.

The task was tackled in different ways. One was that employed by the chieftain of the Cantii whose name has come down to us as 'King Vortigern' (in fact, Vortigern is not a name but a title, meaning, roughly, 'Great Lord'). It is a measure of how deep the incursions from beyond Hadrian's Wall had become that his own tribal territory – what is now Kent at the south-eastern tip of England – was being subjected to them. Lacking sufficient defensive strength among his own people, Vortigern began looking beyond his own frontiers. His eye alighted on the Saxons. Some say that he was invoking the archaic Celtic practice of *celsine* and was trying to place himself in a position of clientship to a stronger people. His fatal error was his failure to appreciate that, not being Celts, the Saxons knew nothing of the strict terms *celsine* laid upon them. On the other hand, he may have believed himself simply to be hiring mercenaries.

In either case, Hengist and Horsa, the two men he introduced to his court, quickly and unscrupulously exploited their advantages, flooded the region with their armed compatriots and, in the end, ousted the Cantian chieftain from his kingdom.

One reason for supposing Vortigern might have been reviving *celsine* is because, in other respects, he was living proof that enclaves of conservative paganism were not limited to the remote north. The contumely he has always received – in Triad 21 he is one of 'the three arrant traitors of the Island of Britain' – is in many ways richly deserved, but his largely Christian critics saw in him a pagan reactionary, and perhaps a potential persecutor.

He employed magicians, and though it is only in the Irish version of Nennius that the magicians at his court are described as Druids, there is every reason to suppose that, even if they did not bear the name, they were playing the same role as the Druids of King Conchobhar. It was they who, when he wanted to build an impregnable fortress against his enemies, advised him that he must first slaughter and bury a fatherless child beneath its foundations. The practice was a common one and seems to have been taken over by the Celts from their predecessors, since the skeletons of children have also been found at some of the stone circles.

According to Geoffrey of Monmouth, Vortigern's chief magician was Merlin, fatherless because his mother conceived him after being seduced by a demon. Geoffrey frequently produces Celtic relics found nowhere else but, unfortunately, they are invariably in a form so garbled as to be merely tantalising. For instance, he tells us how an ancient British king called 'Bellin,' after a series of successful military campaigns on the continent, returned to set up his capital overlooking the Thames. Geoffrey's 'King' Bellin is actually the Celtic sun god Belinus and the place chosen for the royal capital must be Billingsgate, or 'Bellin's gate.' Sadly, although we can draw superficial deductions such as these, he leaves us to speculate as to whether the area was, as seems probable, a centre of the god's cult.

It is much the same in Geoffrey's account of Merlin's birth and one is left wondering whether it does not conceal a misconstrued reference to miraculous births like that of the hero Cu Chulainn. In any event, Geoffrey's Merlin circumvents the fate intended for him by proving to be a greater prophet than the magicians who prescribed it.

However, no matter what Vortigern's intentions may have been, they failed and the Saxon advance continued. His son, who – like his father – is known by title rather than name (that of 'Vortemir' = Great Commander), for a time took up arms against the invaders but was forced remorselessly back towards the west, the region so heavy in symbolism for the Celts.

For many, Arthur represents another way in which the problem of organising local defence forces was tackled, which brings us to the consideration of the historical, as opposed to the mythical, king.

One theory is that Arthur was a professional Roman soldier named Artorius who, after the Roman withdrawal, hired out his services to the British kings, perhaps as leader of a mercenary cavalry unit. Highly mobile, this unit was able to meet the Saxon threat wherever it appeared, though one should not picture its members as resembling the equestrian knights of later times. It was not until the stirrup was copied from the Arabs in the eighth century – an event that marks the beginning of feudalism – that it was possible to fight or engage in any other physical strenuous activity on horseback. Almost certainly they would have fought from chariots.

Numerous alternative theories about the original Arthur have been put forward. In the latter days of Roman occupation, Britain, originally four military provinces, was consolidated into three, the respective commanders holding the titles of *dux Britanniarum* (commander of the Britains), *comes litoris Saxonici* (count of the Saxon shore), and *comes Britanniarum* (count of the Britains). It has been suggested that Arthur may have been the last holder of one or other of these commands. This would mean that, though he need not actually have been a Roman, he would at any rate have been Romanised. It would also help to account for the 'court' attributed to him, for, as a species of imperial viceroy, he would certainly have had something of the sort.

As to the name Artorius, Kenneth Hurlstone Jackson is quite emphatic. It was, he declares, well-known among the Romans and must have passed into British usuage soon after the occupation. Nonetheless, it is strange, as Jean Markale says, that not even Latin writers use any but the British form of it.

Was Arthur a king? The two earliest references to him, in the *Annales Cambriae* and Nennius, which mention the Battle of Mount Badon where the Saxon invaders were defeated do not so describe him. In the first he is not even called the commander of the British forces, while Nennius gives him the title of *dux bellorum,* or war leader. The *dux bellorum* is in keeping with Celtic usage. In a primarily tribal society, whenever combined action by several tribes was necessary – as, for instance, to meet an invasion threat, special measures were taken to minimise jealousies. Nominal command was therefore ascribed, not to any mortal, but to one of the gods whose worship was common to all members of the alliance. It was for this reason that the name 'Brennus', a latinisation of the god-name Bran, occurs twice as a Celtic commander among Roman historians, once as leader of the expedition against Rome and, nearly a century later, against Delphi. There were, however, the physical, day-to-day practicalities of command; the divine general needed his earthly chief of staff. The appointment was decided by a conclave of inter-tribal leaders, who deliberately avoided choosing a king precisely because such a choice might lead to antagonism with rival tribes. The person finally selected was commander for the impending campaign and was, in others words, a *dux bellorum.* The title 'emperor' given to Arthur by Geoffrey of Monmouth is probably just another of his misapprehensions. The Latin *Imperator,* which came to be attached to the political head of the Roman domains, actually means 'giver of orders' (or commander), which is precisely what *dux bellorum* was.

The site of the Battle of Mount Badon, mentioned in the *Annales* and Nennius, remains uncertain, though Bath is the most likely; but its outcome ensured that the Saxon onrush was stayed. The British, though squeezed into one half of their country, were protected behind a fortified line and enjoyed some twenty years of peace

It was the nearest the Celts ever came to unified nationhood during their entire history and, if the historical Arthur ever held real political power, and if he undertook the continental expeditions later ascribed to him, it must have been during this period that he did so.

It was at Camlann – the climax of his dynastic quarrel with Medraut (Mordred) in which both rivals were killed – that it all ended and the way was left open for the Saxons to complete their conquest.

Taking both the documentary and the legendary evidence, there are slightly better grounds for a belief in Arthur's actuality than for regarding him as pure fiction; further weight is given to this by the fact that Arthur became a popular boys' first name in the late sixth and early seventh centuries, a period not long after that in which he would have lived. It also seems likely that he was a native Briton rather than a Roman, and much of the internal evidence suggests he was Cornish rather than Welsh. He is said to have had a court at Kelliwic in Cornwall, while the Battle of Camlann has been tentatively located in the peninsula.[17] But beyond these scanty facts and their interpretation we are in the realm of legend, and before passing on to this an observation about Arthur's Christian credentials should be made.

Although in those eleventh- and twelfth-century lives of the Welsh saints in which he fleetingly figures there is little sign of Arthur's piety, in the *Annales Cambriae* we are told that during the Battle of Mount Badon he carried the cross of 'Our Lord Jesus Christ' for three days and three nights and, in a variant, Nennius says he carried on his shoulder the image of the Virgin Mary.

In the legends he is invariably portrayed as a devoutly Christian prince. Yet immediately we look beneath the superficial declarations we get a whiff of the pagan past. The Siege Perilous at his court is undoubtedly the seat reserved for the Celtic champion and taken by another only if he was prepared to meet its incumbent in single combat. Arthur is also intimately associated with Merlin, a magician of doubtful parentage and as much entitled to be called a Druid as any of Vortigern's or Conchobhar's court. It was Merlin's unscrupulous magic that enabled Arthur's father, Uther Pendragon, to seduce Igerna, the wife of Gorlois. And, at the magician's instance the son of that union established his right to the throne – which was doubtful since he was illegitimate – by the age-old test of the sword in the stone

There is also his somewhat mysterious queen, Guinevere. She has an Irish counterpart in 'Finnabair' daughter of Mebd, certainly a goddess, while according to Malory, Guinevere was the daughter of Sir Leodegrance, generally taken to be a corruption of Ogyr Vran, another form of the name for the British god Bran. She begins to look less like a mortal consort than one of those divine beings to whom, in pagan times, the king was ritually married. This would go some way towards explaining why the Glastonbury epitaph refers to her as a 'second wife,' as pagan kings did have two wives – one immortal, the other mortal.

There is considerable support for Guinevere's Other World nature in the stories. In a passage in Chrétien's 'Perceval' Gawain, at the Castle of the Miracle, is asked about Guinevere by King Arthur's mother. He tells her, in the manner of a wise teacher instructing a pupil, that the queen teaches every living being and that she is the fount and origin of all that is good in the world.

Another aspect typical of Celtic goddesses, that of the 'belle dame sans merci,' is mentioned by Jean Frappier in his essay on Chrétien de Troyes's

---

17   One of the latest and most plausible identifications of Arthur is that provided by Geoffrey Ashe in *The Discovery of King Arthur*. Ashe equates him with a figure called 'Riothamus,' obviously derived from the Celtic word 'Rigotamos,' the Great King, a British ruler who led an army into Gaul in the fifth century and who may have died at Avallon in Burgundy.

'Lancelot or the Knight of the Cart.' She treats her rescuer with icy scorn, refusing to show gratitude and even turning her back on him.[18]

Can we glean from this that the historical Arthur actually fulfilled the pagan custom of marriage to the territorial goddess, or at any rate was credited with having done so? And how can the act be reconciled with his reputation as a Christian prince?

I believe it can be. As I have tried to show, paganism was still an active force in British life in Arthurian times and would therefore have been one which even Romanised and officially Christian rulers would have had to take into account. They would have done so by retaining some of the antique usages. If the Church disapproved in theory it probably had to acquiesce in fact. For one thing it would have been necessary in order to confirm a Christian king's right to rule in the eyes of his only partially converted subjects by showing that he had been chosen and enthroned in accordance with tradition.

As a matter of fact, such customs are still with us. Scottish legend speaks of a stone brought from Ireland and later taken to England. Once it had stood at Tara, where it served as throne during the crowning of the Irish High Kings. Irish legend confirms and tells us that its potency resides in the fact that it was part of the Treasure of the Tuatha De Danann, carried from their native land. It is the Stone of Destiny which now forms part of the Coronation Chair on which British monarchs are crowned.

Besides the need to pay lip-service to tradition, under the pressure of events Christian rulers may well have had to form alliances with non-Christian ones who shared their desire to expel the German invaders. There may well have been ideological compromises on both sides. This may explain how Owein, son of Urien and probably a pagan, is associated with Arthur. It may also offer a clue to a sculpture in the church at Perros showing a bishop standing over Arthur's prone body, while behind is a dead dragon and an unidentified rampantly phallic figure. Extreme sexual potency is frequently associated with Celtic gods like the insatiable Irish Dagda.

There is a second factor which may also help to account for the pagan elements in the stories. This has to do with those who carried the tales from Britain to Europe and with the role myth played in their lives. They were, of course, fugitives – exiled by the Saxon invaders – who established themselves in what in due course came to be called Brittany.

Their depressing and humiliating situation was to some extent redressed by the remembrance and embellishment of glories past and by nursing the dream of its revival. So, in story, there had never been so handsome, so just,

---

18 Keats's poem 'La Belle Dame Sans Merci' is based on the legend of the Irish *banshee*, the beautiful sidh-women who, at Samain, went in search of mortal lovers.

so brave, so generous a king as Arthur. His court was the most splendid in Europe; his knights the bravest. He now lay sleeping in some secret place, one day to awaken and lead his people back to greatness.

More importantly, exile minorities are always under the threat of cultural, and hence racial, absorption by their neighbours. To this danger, mythology has always provided a counter-force, a badge of uniqueness which, in fact, served the colonists well – even today, and despite governmental efforts to suppress it, the Bretons preserve a distinctness often regarded as eccentric by other Frenchmen.

However, it is clear that the stories the refugees took with them included far more than that which, strictly speaking, can be classified as within the Arthurian canon. Much of it must have been much earlier, pre-Christian matter. No doubt carried away by their enthusiasm for the king and his knights, a gradual change took place in non-Arthurian matter. In some cases, this amounted to little more than awarding a knighthood to a pagan god, so that Ogyr Vran becomes 'Sir Leodegrance', father of Guinevere. In other cases, the change is more complete, as is well exemplified in *Kulhwch*. Not only does it have its long list of characters, including pagan heroes and gods who are now members of King Arthur's court, but also its central boar-hunt, a theme that can be traced back to Indo-European roots.

Over the years countless attempts to equate the Arthurian characters with a variety of gods have been, and no doubt will continue to be made. Squires's 'Artaius' at least has the merit of being Celtic, but Arthur has also been identified as the Norse Thor and the Greek Apollo. All seem to me equally doomed to failure and the most we can say with confidence is that Arthur, in many ways, resembles the Irish solar-heroes like Cu Chulainn or Finn mac Cumhail and that his knightly retinue may be seen as the medieval counterpart of those bands, like the Fianna, who figure in the Fenian cycle.

It is far more likely that the Breton storytellers, aware of what most interested their listeners, displaced, or at any rate renamed, a whole host of earlier gods and heroes to make the British king and the members of his court the focal centre of their material. In other words these latter-day myth-makers used an existing tradition as the foundation on which they constructed their own.

Chapter 13

THE ROYAL COMPANY

Despite the changes it underwent, there is no doubt that the Arthurian stories retain much that stems from the distant past. As many of these relics are not to be found anywhere else, they not only confirm the extreme antiquity of the material from which the Breton storytellers worked, but also give further evidence that the mythology is a reflection of Druidism. Accordingly they are of significance in any attempt to build up a picture of the Celtic supernatural and some of them will be examined in the following pages.

THE GRAIL AND THE SPEAR. The grail episode has always been one of the most mysterious in the entire Arthurian canon, inspiring countless retellings, in particular those in which its symbols have been Christianised.

It has also been the subject of innumerable 'interpretations.' Among the most famous and, in its time, influential – its symbolism was adopted by T. S. Eliot in *The Waste Land* – was that of Jessie Weston, elucidated in *From Ritual to Romance*. In her view the episode derived from the archaic agriculturist myth of the vegetation god who is wounded, dies, is buried and finally resurrected, the successive events symbolising the decline in the earth's fertility in winter and its revival in spring.

In spite of the euphemisms often employed in the myths, the cause of the hero's death is undoubtedly a wound to the genitals; in other words, one which affects his sexual virility and, the fecundity of the earth being associated with his own, it is this loss which turns it into a Waste Land, the barren landscape of winter. Thus, in Jessie Weston's view, the Lame King, whose land is in this condition, has suffered such a wound, while the spear and the chalice are to be seen as symbols for phallus and uterus, representations of which played a part in the ritual enactments of the vegetation myth almost universally.

It is true that, in many ways, the grail resembles the cornucopiae or horns of plenty often associated with the Great Mother, and these are usually taken to represent the organ whereby increase comes about – her boundless womb. In support of Jessie Weston's thesis, it should be said that horns of plenty are associated with Celtic goddesses in a number of artefacts. For example, a relief of Epona found near Puy-de-Dome in France shows her, not only with her horse-attribute, but also with a cornucopia. The goddess represented on a 30-inch high statuette from Lydney in Gloucester holds a similar object, and on a relief from Bewcastle in Cumberland is a seated goddess who has fruits piled on her lap. In other words, several of the elements of the classical vegetation myth are to be found in the grail episode.

Jessie Weston believed that the story of the Dying God, already deeply embedded in the human psyche, was in due course syncretised with that of Christ's death, burial, and resurrection to become the central rite of an esoteric Christian cult, later suppressed as heretical. Its relics are to be found in grail stories as told by the various authors, some of whom – she specifies the Burgundian Robert De Boron – may have known of or even been members of the heretical cult.

Her argument is pitted with flaws, now too well known to need rehearsal. For one thing, the Celtic cornucopia-holding figures mentioned all date from Gallo-Roman times and so were probably influenced by the classical imagery; and as to her esoteric cult, we have no evidence it ever existed to be suppressed.

In any case, the Dying God myth and the grail story are materially different. It is true that the Lame King's infirmity is probably due to a genital wound. It is also true that down to late times the Celts believed royal virility and the fertility of the land were linked. In Walter Map's late twelfth century *De nugis curialium,* it is stated that no animals would bear their young in the parish where Alan of Brittany had been castrated and crossed into the next parish when the time for delivery arrived.

Yet there is a missing ingredient: the Dying God is invariably rescued from the underworld by a woman – be she his mother, wife, sister, or lover. Nothing in the grail episode implies anything of the kind. In fact, hints of something far more like a Celtic vegetation myth are to be found elsewhere, in the incident of Pryderi and the Castle of the Golden Bowl, where it is his mother Rhiannon who tries to rescue him. But in the Golden Bowl incident we have no whisper of a Lame King, no spear, and the golden bowl itself bears little resemblance to the grail.

It is not until the British 'Peredur' that we find these components coming together. Like the Castle of the Golden Bowl, the castle in which this story takes place is one of those typical Celtic Other World ones which the hero comes upon after passing through 'a great forest.' There the similarities cease.

Before his arrival, Peredur has been warned that, whatever strange sights he sees in the castle, he is to ask no questions; later he is rather unjustly reproached for his restraint and told that had he asked the right question the Lame King would have been healed.

Much the same happens in Chrétien's 'Perceval,' though in this the hero awakens next morning to find the castle deserted, while in the first Continuation Gauvain (Gawain) – partly successful in his quest in that he asks the vital question – finds himself next morning lying on a cliff above the sea. As he rides away he sees that the Waste Kingdom has been restored.

Perceval's experience is very similar to one in the Irish 'Baile in Scail', the earliest surviving recension of which is dated to the mid eleventh century. Here King Conn is invited by a phantom horseman to his dwelling where he sees a crowned maiden, the Sovereignty of Ireland; her husband, the horseman, reveals himself as Lugh. She first serves their guest with enormous helpings of meat, then begins to pour ale. As she does so she keeps asking Lugh: 'To whom shall his cup be given?' He answers with the names of future kings. When he has finished, house and dwellers vanish. Apart from the other similarities the question Lugh's wife repeats suggests the one Perceval should have asked; Who is to be served from this?

The correspondence is clinched by a further detail: in one passage in the Irish tales Lugh's wife, the Sovereignty of Ireland, assumes a repellant shape, as does the grail-bearer in 'Peredur' when she reappears to explain the significance of the sights he has seen.

The spear which both Peredur and Perceval are shown, and which was later equated with that of Longinus, the centurion who pierced the side of Christ, is also connected with Lugh in the Irish Matter. In one passage his magic spear drips blood when held aloft and in another is described as being carried in front of a cauldron of blood.

In both 'Peredur' and 'Perceval' the denouement is implausible and does not correspond with the previously stated facts. For example, Perceval is told that the platter contains food for the Fisher King's father, 'not a pike, a lamprey, or a salmon he received, but a single mass wafer.' Unable to leave his chamber for the past fifteen years on account of his infirmity, this has been his sole sustenance. More questions are raised than answered thereby. Why, for instance, is a mass-wafer measuring about two inches in diameter served on a dish long enough for a salmon, and not on a liturgical vessel? Why is the server, not a priest, but a woman? And why does Chrétien stress that the dish was being used for a purpose other than for its normal one of serving fish?

The fact that the explanations in 'Peredur' and 'Perceval' fail to provide answers to so many of the fundamental questions raised by the sights both see has led some commentators to believe that (1) at least in part; the author of 'Peredur' has borrowed from the French source, and (2) that there must have been an earlier version offering a more satisfactory explanation. Either the later redactor did not really understand the meaning of the incident or else it was too manifestly pagan to fit into the Christianised version he was trying to create. To decipher the incident, therefore, it we have to seek elsewhere.

The word translated as 'platter' is the Welsh word *dyscyl*. This would be an apt rendering of what later came to be called a grail, a word derived from *gradalis,* a long flat dish used for serving fish and familiar in monasteries during the Friday fasts. Hence, Chrétien's reference to it as one on which fish was served.

But the same word is actually the one used in 'The Thirteen Treasures' to describe the vessel of Rhydderch from which 'whatever food was wished for was immediately provided'; and in the Manessier Continuation of 'Perceval' we are told that after the grail's passage the tables were filled with magnificent dishes so that 'no man could name a food he could not find there.' This identifies it as one of the recurrent magic cauldrons of Celtic lore with their characteristics of inexhaustibility and restoring life. In fact, later in the same story, the Peredur actually sees one with the second capacity. Of course, what Peredur is shown only partially corresponds with what Perceval saw, for, in the former case, the platter does not contain a mass wafer but a severed head lying amid a welter of blood. And this I believe to be our best key to the interpretation of the incident.

Miraculous heads appear in both the Irish and British Matter, with that of Bran among the best known. One might hazard a guess that it is his which is involved here, for like the king in Peredur, Bran suffered a wound to the thighs. Indeed, in the *Didot Leval* the Fisher King is named as Bron.

The wound and its nature might seem to argue in favour of Jessie Weston's hypothesis: that it is the cause of the blight on the land. It would do so if loss of sexual potency were the only thing which, in Celtic belief, could lead to such a result. But it was not. It could also come about when the cosmic equilibrium is disturbed and will continue as long as no attempt is made to restore it. The story makes clear that just such a disturbance had taken place and that it had been in Peredur's power to end it, for he is told later that the head was that of a slain kinsman (the bleeding spear is presumably the murder weapon). Had he asked, he would have been given this information. He would have been forced to recognise his own inescapable duty – to avenge the death.

In the Celtic code an unavenged murder was a 'sin crying to heaven for vengeance.' And it was because it was not avenged that the king remained lame or impotent and his realm barren. The symbolical meaning of the fields of black and white sheep that Peredur sees now becomes clear and apposite: standing for the essential balance between the two worlds, they serve as a reminder to Peredur of the need to restore it when it has been broken.

THE MYSTERIOUS GAMES IN 'GEREINT.'

Although less well known, the meaning of the incident of the games in 'Gereint' is as strange as that of the grail episode.

Since the knight who approaches in response to Enid's scream as her husband falls from his horse is called 'Death,' and since she asks the Little

King what fame he can gain by killing a dead man, there can be no doubt that what follows takes place in the Other World.

Tolstoy sees in the games a reference to Lugnasad, the feast of Lugh. The horn which Gereint is instructed to blow to end them is hanging from an apple tree, and Lugnasad took place in August when apples are in fruit. Furthermore, that it should commemorate the god's liberation from the underworld would be consistent with the vegetation myths of other societies, and, as we have seen, in several parts of the Celtic world Lugnasad was associated with the corn harvest.

Evidence that Chrétien's 'Erec,' which contains the same incident, was derived from Welsh sources not available to the writer of 'Gereint' is that he names the knight who challenges the hero in the brocade pavilion as 'Mabonograin,' plainly a debased from of 'Mabon ap Modron,' who has been identified as Lugh. As Mabon, he is the prisoner whom the companions in 'Kulhwch' have to liberate and we have seen the parallels between him and Pryderi, also equated with Lugh, in the Castle of the Golden Bowl. One is therefore led to wonder whether the 'Gereint' incident is not the true ending of the incident in 'Manawydan.' It would certainly make a great deal more sense than the existing one.

The word 'Lugnasad' has been translated in two ways. One gives 'the assemblies of Lugh'; the other, 'the games of Lugh.' The latter suggests that his feast was marked by games, possibly ritualistic, possibly actual athletic contests, like the Pythian Games dedicated to Apollo. It may well have been that games of which those in the 'Gereint' incident are a relic formed part of the Lugnasad celebrations. However, Loomis believes that the suffix – 'nasad' actually means 'marriage' and that Lugnasad was a time when young men and women gathered for the purpose of match-making.

This, too, would accord with vegetation myth, in many versions of which an additional reason for celebrating the god's liberation is that it reunites him with his grieving lover. In the commemorative festivals of some cultures this was marked by offering him a mortal bride, the most beautiful girl in the community, who was of course a sacrificial victim, but such a time was also one of general match-making.

Guinevere and Lancelot. If Guinevere belongs to the Other World, as suggested in the last chapter, it would help to explain why Lancelot has to cross the Perilous Bridge, the classic shamanistic link between the two domains, to find and rescue her. Guinevere is thus the abducted goddess who, like Sita, wife of Rama in the Hindu *Ramayana,* occurs in many mythologies.

But Lancelot's rivalry to Arthur also brings to mind those fickle transfers of favour often exhibited by Celtic goddesses. Can it be the young knight has become a candidate for the kingship, perhaps because Arthur is now ageing and she is losing interest in him? In Chrétien he actually undergoes successfully the same trial by which Arthur established his royal claim – one involving an immense stone.

Although there are dissimilarities – for example, there is no embedded sword and the stone is actually the lid of the sarcophagus destined to house his mortal remains – one can only agree with Robert Graves that a trial involving the lifting of a stone was a traditional Indo-European test of kingship. Odin has to undergo it and a scene involving a sword and a rock is shown on a Hittite carving, while the royalty of Theseus, king of Athens is established when he recovers the sword his father Aegeus has deposited beneath a boulder. What is more, by lifting the stone Lancelot is said to have proved himself to be the prophesised liberator of those now held prisoner, and 'The Liberator' was often one of the titles of kings.

Although it is possible that, in keeping with Celtic tradition, the real Arthur may have undergone some kind of ritual marriage to the territorial deity, the most likely explanation for the Lancelot-Guinevere material is that it is of earlier provenance and that the name of an Arthurian knight was attached to it in post-Christian times. At the same time, in keeping with the Christian morality, their relationship becomes one of heinous adultery.

The queen's involvement with Lancelot is only one of three of what might be called her 'extra-marital relationships.' Besides Lancelot, there is the one with her abductor Melwas (Meleagant) – which is, to say the least, ambiguous – and her later one with Medraut (Mordred), which causes the Battle of Camlann and Arthur's death. On the assumption that Guinevere is actually a territorial goddess, her liaisons might be said to illustrate the need for the king to be ever watchful over his divine spouse. As we known from Mebd in the Tain, these divine ladies 'never had one man without another waiting in his shadow.'

The transfer of Guinevere's affections to Mordred suggests that Arthur failed in this respect, but it is comprehensible in terms of Celtic belief. Mordred had been appointed regent while the king was campaigning abroad. During this time he would need the goodwill of its tutelary deity on behalf of his people. The quarrel between king and nephew is provoked by his unwillingness to return her.

MERLIN. Of all the characters in Arthurian Legend Merlin is surely the strangest and the one who most unmistakably seems to wear the marks of the past. He is another of those court druids, like Cathbad and Mag Roth, even though, according to Malory, he advises churchmen like the Archbishop of Canterbury.

Is he to be taken as another sign that, under its Christian exterior, the court of the historical Arthur was actually deeply imbued with the pagan past? We could only be certain if we could associate Merlin indisputably with it, or at least if we could show he was present in the earliest versions of the legends. We cannot do so because the first time the character ultimately to become Merlin appears is in Nennius. There he is named as Ambrosius and is not linked with the historical Arthur. Nor does any such linkage occur until centuries later.

Gerald of Wales says that there were two Merlins. The earliest was the Merlin Ambrosius, mentioned by Nennius, who, as Myrddin, is supposed to have given the city of Carmarthen its name. He was contemporary with Vortigern and provided Geoffrey of Monmouth with his 'Merlin.' The other, born in Scotland, was first surnamed Celidonius, after the Celidonian (or Caledonian) Forest where he prophesied, but was later called Sylvester because during a battle he saw a terrible monster in the sky and as a result went mad, so that, till his death, he lived the life of a wild animal. It was this Merlin, Gerald says, who lived in the time of Arthur, though even here he is not explicitly associated with the king.

Gerald's attempts at elucidation have simply muddled things. We have seen that there is no real basis for the belief that Merlin or Myrrdin gave his name to Carmarthen. Besides, among the texts in the Ancient Books are poems bearing the name 'Myrddin.' Geoffrey's Merlin is supposedly contemporary with Vortigern, but the author must have drawn on the Myrddin poems in his *Vita Merlini,* for place and personal names from them occur in it. But the poems themselves make clear that the wild man of the Caledonian Forest and the writer of the poems quoted are the same. One, 'The Appletree,' actually refers both to a battle and to his living in 'the Forest of Celyddon.'

Who then is he? The patron saint of Glasgow is Kentigern and a twelfth-century life mentions a madman, Laloecen, also associated with places named in the Myrddin poems and Geoffrey. A fifteenth-century manuscript in the British Library (MS Cotton Titus, A. xix) has similar as well as additional details. During a battle, it says, warrior hosts began appearing in the sky. A man named as 'Lailoken' was accused of being responsible for the slaughter of the battle and, as a result, went mad, deserted the habitations of men, and lived the life of a forest animal. St. Kentigern learns the story when he encounters him by chance and is later instrumental in reconciling the madman with the Church just before the death he has prophesied for himself. This takes place when he is stoned and beaten by shepherds, impaled on a sharp spike, and thrown into the Tweed, thereby fulfilling his prophesy that he would die in three ways.

Since the milieux are the same in all cases there can be little doubt that this is Merlin Sylvester. 'Laloecen' and 'Lailoken' are misreadings of the Welsh word *Llallogan*, dear friend, which has been converted from a salutation into a name.

In Geoffrey, Merlin is not mentioned after his involvement in Arthur's adulterous conception and it is not until the time of Robert de Boron, at the turn of the twelfth century, that the magician is more firmly attached to Arthur, while it was as late as the time of Malory, in the fifteenth century, that he becomes a permanent royal adviser.

Tolstoy sees Myrddin, the Caledonian Forest madman, as a surviving relic of the past, convincingly associates him with the cults of gods like Cernunnos and Lugh, and suggests he may have been a royal bard.[19] This is further evidence, not only of the survival of the cults of pagan gods through the Roman era, but in all likelihood of a later revival after their departure. Even his demise in three forms recalls the Celtic triple death which, as Tolstoy says, may have been that which Lleu/Lugh is supposed to have undergone at the hands of Blodeuwedd and Goronwy in the 'Math ap Mathonwy.' But the fact that Merlin Sylvester's killers are said to have been 'shepherds' may also be significant, in view of the fact that the old ways survived most tenaciously among country people Was his, then, a ritual sacrifice of which he was the willing victim, a situation not unknown in Celticism? This would certainly explain how he was able to predict his death so accurately.

Yet however confidently we can establish that Arthur's Merlin derives from the madman of the Caledonian Forest we are still left with an unanswerable conundrum: how does it come about that this figure, so much like a court Druid, does not find his way into the royal household until the fifteenth-century, long after Druidism has departed the scene? And what is he doing as adviser of a king who, in every other respect, is the very paragon of Christian virtue?

THE OTHER COMPANIONS. The themes and characters of the Arthurian legends have been the subject of books and articles beyond count and in the limited space available I can limit myself only to those appearing in the earliest texts.

Of the remaining knightly companions the ones most closely associated with the king, besides his queen and Merlin, are Kai (Kay) and Bedwyr (Bedivere), who first appear in 'Kulhwch.'

Both are markedly Celtic. Kai, presented as a boaster, given to moods of surliness, and with the capacity of provoking quarrels round him is in these respects like the Irish Bricriu who made almost a profession of setting people at odds with one another.

Unlike Bricriu, Kai has the reputation for being an outstanding warrior whose sword 'never left his hand in battle.' What is more, the sword itself has the magical property that no doctor could cure a wound it inflicted. He is thus the archetypal Celtic hero and, like others, is credited with extreme good looks – in 'The Dream of Rhonabwy' he is called 'the most handsome

---

19 Rolleston in *Myths and Legends of the Celtic Race* also links him with the god Nuada/Llud.

man in Arthur's kingdom.' Also in the manner of Celtic heroes, he has supernatural gifts. He can hold his breath under water for nine days and nights, can do without sleep for the same period, and can stretch himself out until he is as tall as the tallest tree in the forest. These can only be compared with the changes Cu Chulainn is able to bring about in himself, particularly when in his warrior-fury.

The aura of the supernatural also surrounds Kai's inseparable companion, Bedwyr, another great warrior and also a man of outstanding good looks. The one characteristic which sets him apart from Kai is that he is one handed, bringing to mind Nuada/Llud. Equations between the two have, naturally, been made, though on the available evidence they are not totally convincing.

At the same time, the fact that Kai and Bedwyr so invariably form a trio with Arthur has led Markale to suggest they may represent Dumezil's trilogy of Indo-European deities. Again, the equation is dubious.

Markale also lists Gawain (Gwalchmei in the *Mabinogion*), allegedly Arthur's nephew, as among his boon companions and it is in this role that he appears in 'Kulhwch,' 'Owein,' 'Peredur,' and 'Gereint.' In the last he is named as the most favoured of nine captains on account of his fame, fighting ability, and noble bearing. In 'Owein' we have him, as the king's chosen companion, consoling him over Owein's long absence from the court, and even venturing to offer advice. In the Triads he is eulogised as one of the three golden-tongued knights of Arthur's court, 'so wise, so fair and gentlemanly in their deportment; so eloquent and sweetly spoken that it was difficult to refuse them anything they desired' (Triad 115). It is no doubt for this reason that Arthur chose him to conduct the most delicate negotiations, including those involving Isolt's honour when King Mark questions it.

Like Kai and Bedwyr, Gawain is endowed with magical abilities. For though he rises in the morning with the 'strength of a good knight,' it constantly doubles through the morning and continues to do so until midnight. We here have a hint of something not associated with Arthur's other two companions, who may have been actual members of the real Arthur's warrior band that later passed into myth. Gawain's waxing strength through the day suggests a solar god.

The last three of those who are the king's closest companions are, in the oldest texts, Owein/Yvain, Yder/Edern, and Gwynn.

Owein, the son of Urien, is the eponymous hero of the half-realistic, half-fantastical story of the Countess of the Fountain in which, among other adventures, he encounters the black giant identified as the horned-god Cernunnos.

In 'The Dream of Rhonabwy,' full of mysterious allusions, Owein has a troop of ravens which seem to be involved in some kind of battle with

Arthur's forces. Markale links the birds with Modron who, as the Morrigan of the Irish stories, had the capacity to turn herself into a raven. The fact that it is a bird of carrion has always led to its association with the battlefield. The collocation 'glutting the ravens' was a metaphor used by the Norse skalds for slaughter and, even in late times, the sight of a flock of them wheeling in the sky was taken by armies on the march as the presage of a coming encounter with the enemy.

Owein's father, Urien, himself appears in stories, where he is variously named as King Uriens or Urience of Gore, King Rience or Ryons of the North, and even as King Nentres of Garloth.

Yder/Edern is a killer of giants and bears. The first recalls the Norse Thor, whose magic hammer Mjollnir was used for precisely this purpose. The bear occurs in Celtic artefacts and proper names. Math, for example, means 'bear' and the existence of the bear element Art- in Arthur has led to speculation that he, too, derives from a bear god.

Yder it is who insults Guinevere and so provokes Gereint/Erec to pursue and defeat him in single combat. He also has a brother, Gwynn, who as Gwynn ap Nudd is associated with the underworld. His name would identify him with the Irish Finn, as both mean 'white' or 'fair', though there is nothing else to link them.

As to Gereint, like Peredur, he may have been based on a real figure, possibly a seventh-century Cornish knight.

Other figures who appear in some of the later versions can be readily recognised as gods. For example, Malory's Balin and Balan are a doublet of the sun god Belinus, who is probably also the Pelles and the Little King in 'Gereint' and 'Erec.'

Bran appears not only as Sir Leodegrance, father of Guinevere, but also as King Brandegore or Brandegoris (Bran of Gower), as Sir Brandel or Brandiles (Bran of Gwales), as Uther Pendragon (Uther Pen = Wonderful or Terrible Head). In his guise of Bran the Blessed (Bran Vendigeit) he has been corrupted into King Ban of Benwyk. He is also the 'Sir Breunor' who, in Malory, challenges Sir Tristram and is decapitated by him, just as Bran undergoes voluntary decapitation.

An exhaustive discussion of all the pagan elements in the Arthur matter would require an entire book of its own and the foregoing is intended only to delineate landmarks and has, I am aware, left unsolved innumerable mysteries. One can only hope, on the other hand, that it has helped to demonstrate the persistence of material going back, not centuries, but millennia.

It is part of the extraordinary character of the Arthurian stories that such apparently alien and certainly un-Christian matter can fall so naturally into its new milieu that it is as if it always belonged there.

Chapter 14

EPILOGUE
CELTIC MYTH AND US

It is the adaptability, not only of the Arthurian matter, but of the rest of Celtic mythology that is one of the measures of its literary greatness, for it is only literature of such stature that – like *The Epic of Gilgamesh,* the *Iliad,* the *Odyssey, or Beowulf* – possesses that kind of vital resilience that speaks to so many human conditions. It is for precisely this reason that it has been such an enormous influence on all subsequent literature, making the task of trying to describe it exceptionally difficult. None, not even the Greek, has been so deep or so widespread.

Nor so timeless. As Arthurian legend inspired the troubadours and the Breton *lais*-singers, as well as medieval writers like Geoffrey, Wace, Layamon, Chrétien de Troyes, Wolfram von Eschenbach, and Marie de France, so it provided the basic inspiration for Spenser's *Faerie Queene* in the sixteenth century and Alain-Fournier's *Le Grand Meaulnes* in the twentieth.

Traces of Celtic myth are to be found in Chaucer and Shakespeare, in *The Tempest* and *As You Like It.* They are to made out in Racine and Corneille and even Molière. Its themes were picked up and developed by Scott, Tennyson, Swinburne, Arnold, and Hardy. John Cowper Powys used them in *Porius;* T. H. White in The *Sword in the Stone.* Of recent years we have had the musical *Camelot* and John Boorman's film *Excalibur.*

What is true of the British Matter is true of the Matter of Ireland. Macpherson's *Ossianic Ballads* may be works of the writer's imagination rather than mythology in the strict sense, but Oisin's visit to Tir na n'Og is treated in W. B. Yeats's *Wanderings of Oisin*, while J. M. Synge also adapted native Celtic themes.

And they turn up in the most unexpected places. The *Chansons de Geste,* very much in the knightly tradition, purport to present historical events that have nothing whatever to do with the Celts. Yet the 'Ganelon' who appears in Beroul's *Tristan and Iseut* as one of 'the three villains' plays a similar role in the twelfth-century *Chanson de Roland.* Identification is hazardous but he may possibly be the British Gwydion in much altered form. Markale has discovered other examples in *Roland.* Another villain, 'Guenes,' is Gwynn, son of Nuada of the Silver Hand, while Guenes's uncle 'Guinemer' is, notwithstanding the change of sex, none other than Guinevere. The saracen Tervagant is surely the Tarvos Trigarannos (= Bull with Three Cranes) found at Notre de Dame de Paris in the eighteenth century and dated to the first century AD, Tervagant also comes into the *Chanson d'Apremont*, together with Balan, identified by Markale as the solar deity Belinus.

It is as if the mythology has truly entered the western psyche, haunting and addressing itself to all ages and to all situations. It continues at a rate which would render any list provided here out of date in the interval between the writing and the publication of this book.

As to those motifs which are so recurrent, literature is unimaginable without them. The woman betrothed against her will and in love with another is the very stuff of romance. The duel of heroes, like those between Cu Chulainn and the Connaught champions, is repeated in countless Westerns. Underwater cities have figured in many science-fiction stories and may even have provided the basis for the legends of the lost continents Mantis and Lemuria. A submarine locale figures in 'The Dalkey Archive' by the contemporary Irish writer Flann O'Brien, while the surreal comedy that haunts his work, and which can be found in myths such as *Da Datho's Pig*, has found expression even on television in 'Monty Python's Flying Circus.'

The Celtic attitude to time, which could lead Breton storytellers to begin with the formula 'Once upon a time when there was no time,' is found in Joyce and others of the 'stream of consciousness' and 'non-linear' schools of writing. Markale detects it in Alain Robbe-Grillet, himself a Breton and one of the founding-fathers of Roman Nouveau.

In the realm of fairy stories the Celtic influence has been particularly strong. Many of Perrault's *Contes* are derived from Breton, and therefore Celtic, folk-tales, which themselves derive from the stories of the Tuatha De Danann. In our own century, Tolkien's *Lord of the* Rings breathes the very atmosphere of the Celtic Other World and even has its Druids in the form of the magicians Gandulf and Saruman.

Besides prose, Celtic mythology also haunts poetry. Baudelaire and Apollinaire frequently write in the bardic vein. The poems of Dylan Thomas, such as 'The Force that Through the Green Fuse,' are living echoes of Amergin and of Taliessin's 'War of the Trees.'

One thing can be said with conviction: whatever sacred role the myths may have played in paganism, there can be no doubt that they have provided us with a classical literature, an inspiration on which we are likely to continue drawing.

What is the essence of Celtic mythology that makes it so perennially influential? Mythology, as has been observed elsewhere, is history in other terms. But it is also a particular kind of history. It is history as it ought to be, not as it was. Historians, ever searching for the truth, however distasteful to nations or to humanity in general, would – perhaps rightly – disapprove. There is something to be said for it, all the same. If we can preserve the illusion of past Golden Ages, we can also maintain what may also be illusion: that such ages are recoverable or may be achieved in the future. It is that which sustains us throughout life.

One day we may all of us find our Tir na n'Og.

Select Bibliography

Ashe, Geoffrey, *The Ancient Wisdom* (London, 1977).

——, *The Discovery of King Arthur* (London, 1985).

Atkinson, Robert, *The Book of Ballymote* (Dublin, 1887).

——, *The Book of Leinster* (Dublin, 1880).

Beroul, *The Romance of Tristan*, tr. Alan S. Fedrick (London, 1982).

Caesar, Gaius Julius, *The Conquest of Gaul*, tr. S. A. Handford (Harmondsworth, 1951).

Campbell, Joseph, *Oriental Mythology* (New York, 1973).

——, Creative Mythology (New York, 1968).

——, Myths to Live By (New York, 1960).

——, Primitive Mythology (London, 1974).

Castleden, Rodney, *The Wilmington Giant* (Wellingborough, 1983).

Celtic Miscellany, A, tr. K. H. Jackson (Harmondsworth, 1951).

Chadwick, Nora, *The Celts* (Harmondsworth, 1970).

Chrétien (de Troyes), *Arthurian Romances* tr. W. W. Comfort (London, 1975).

Cormac, *Cormac's Glossary,* tr. John O'Donovan (Calcutta, 1868).

Cunliffe, Barry, *The Regni* (London, 1973).

Davidson, H. R. Ellis, *Gods and Myths of Northern Europe* (Harmondsworth, 1977).

Death of Arthur, The, tr. James Cable (Harmondsworth, 1971).

Detsicas, Alec, *The Cantiaci* (London, 1973).

Dillon, Myles, *Early Irish Literature* (Chicago, 1972).

——, with Nora Chadwick, *The Celtic Realms* (London, 1972).

Dunnett, Rosalind, *The Trinovantes* (London, 1973).

Earliest English Poems, The, tr. Michael Alexander (Harmondsworth, 1966).

Early Irish Myths and Sagas ed. Jeffrey Gantz (Harmondsworth, 1981).

Eliade, Mircea, *Images and Symbols* (Paris, 1969).

——, *Shamanism: Archaic Technique of Ecstasy* (Paris, 1951).

Evans, J. Gwenogvryn, *Facsimile of the Black Book of Carmarthen* (Oxford, 1888).

——, *The Text of the Bruts from the Red Book of Hergest* (Oxford, 1890).

——, *The Text of the 'Mabinogion' and the other Welsh tales from the Red Book of Hergest* (Oxford. 1893).

Fox, Aileen, *The Dumnonii* (London, 1973).

Frankfort, Henri and others, *Before Philosophy* (Chicago, 1946).

Frappier, Jean, article in Arthurian *Literature in the Middle Ages*, ed. R. S. Loomis (Oxford, 1959).

Frazer, Sir J. G., *The Golden Bough* (Harmondsworth, 1978).

Geoffrey (of Monmouth), *The History of the Kings of Britain* (Harmondsworth, 1966).

———, *Vita Merlin*, ed. Basil Clarke (Cardiff, 1973).

Gerald of Wales, *The History and Topography of Ireland* (Harmondsworth, 1951).

———, *The Journey through Wales: Description of Wales* (Harmondsworth, 1978).

Graves, Robert, *The White Goddess* (London, 1977).

———, *The Greek Myths,* 2 vols. (Harmondsworth, 1984).

Guest, Lady Charlotte, *The Mabinogion* (London, 1849).

Harrier, Michael, *The Way of the Shaman* (San Francisco, 1980).

Hatto, A. T., *Shamanism and Epic Poetry* (London, 1970).

Herm, Gerhard, *The Celts* (London, 1976).

Holy Grail, The Quest for the, tr. P. M. Matarasso (Harmondsworth, 1969).

Hooke, S. H., *Middle Eastern Mythology* (Harmondsworth, 1963).

Hoyle, F., 'Stonehenge: An Eclipse Predictor,' article in *Nature* (London, 1966).

———, 'Speculations on Stonehenge,' article in *Antiquity* (London, 1966).

Jackson, K. H., article in *Arthurian Literature in the Middle Ages* (Oxford, 1959).

Jubainville, H. d'Arbois de, *Le cycle mythologique irlandais et la mythologic celtique* (Paris, 1884).

Jung, C. G. and others, *Man and His Symbols* (London, 1964).

Kendrick. T. D., *The Druids: A Study in Prehistory* (London, 1927),

Kirk, G. S. *The Nature of Greek Myths* (Harmondsworth, 1974).

Kerenyi, C., *Gods of the Greeks* (London, 1976).

Layamon, *Brut,* tr. Eugene Mason (London, 1977).

Lewis, I. M., *Ecstatic Religion* (Harmondsworth, 1971).

Lommel, A., *Shamanism: The Beginning of Art* (New York and Toronto, 1974).

Loomis, R. S. (ed.), *Arthurian Literature in the Middle Ages* (Oxford, 1959).

———, article in *Funk and Wagnall's Dictionary of Folklore, Mythology and Legend* (London, 1975).

Mabinogion, The, ed. Jeffrey Gantz (Harmondsworth, 1976).

Malory, Thomas, *The Morte d'Arthur,* ed. Janet Cowen (Harmondsworth, 1984).

Markale, Jean, *Le Roi Arthur* (Paris, 1976).

——, *Women of the Celts* (London, 1975).

——, *Les Celtes et la civilisation celtique* (Paris, 1975).

——, *Le druidisme* (Paris, 1985).

Martin, M., *A Description of the Western Islands of Scotland* (London, 1703).

Morganwg, Iolo, *The Triads of Britain,* ed. Malcolm Smith (London, 1977).

Nennius, *Historia Brittonum,* ed. Theodor Mommsen (Berlin, 1894).

Piggott, Stuart, *The Druids* (Harmondsworth, 1974).

Pindar, *The Odes,* tr. C. M. Bowra (Harmondsworth, 1985).

Powell, T. G. E., *The Celts* (London, 1958).

Rhys, John, *Celtic Folklore* (London, 1901).

Rolleston, T. W., *Myths and Legends of the Celtic Race* (London, 1911).

Ross, Anne, Pagan *Celtic Britain* (London, 1974).

Rutherford, Ward, *The Druids* (Wellingborough, 1985).

——, *Pythagoras: Lover of Wisdom* (Wellingborough, 1984).

——, *Shamanism* (Wellingborough, 1986).

Sayers, Dorothy L., *The Song of Roland* (Harmondsworth, 1957).

Sir Gawain and the Green Knight, tr. Brian Stone (Harmondsworth, 1959).

Skene, William F., *The Four Ancient Books of Wales* (Edinburgh, 1868).

Squires, Charles, *The Mythology of the British Islands* (London, 1905).

Stephens, Thomas, *The Gododdin of Aneurin Gwawdrydd* (London, 1888).

Tain [Bo Cuailnge], The, tr. Thomas Kinsella (Oxford, 1970).

Tierney, J. J., *The Celtic Ethnography of Posidonius* (Dublin, 1960).

Todd, Malcolm, *The Corintani* (London, 1973).

Tolstoy, Nikolai, *The Quest for Merlin* (London, 1985).

Wace of Jersey, *The Roman de Brut,* tr. Eugene Mason (London, 1962).

Weber, Max, *The Religion of India* (London, 1958).

Weston, Jessie L., *From Ritual to Romance* (Cambridge, 1920).

Wood, John Edwin, *Sun, Moon and Standing Stone* (Oxford, 1978).

INDEX